✧ *Companions for the Journey* ✧

Praying with
Clare of Assisi

D0923919

✧ *Companions for the Journey* ✧

Praying with Clare of Assisi

by
Ramona Miller, OSF
and
Ingrid Peterson, OSF

the WORD
among us®

To our Rochester Franciscan Sisters
✧ *whose generosity reveals to us* ✧
Clare's vision of community

The psalm on page 51 (second excerpt) is from *Psalms Anew,* compiled by Nancy Schreck and Maureen Leach (Winona, MN: Saint Mary's Press, 1986), page 53. Copyright © 1986 by Saint Mary's Press. All rights reserved.

The scriptural material found on pages 33, 38, 44, 56, 60, 71, and 81 is freely adapted and is not to be understood or used as an official translation of the Bible.

All other scriptural quotations used in this book are from the New Jerusalem Bible. Copyright © 1985 by Darton, Longman & Todd, Ltd., London; and Doubleday, a division of Random House, Inc. Used with permission.

10 09 08 07 06   5 6 7 8 9

The acknowledgments continue on page 113.

Printed in the United States of America
ISBN 0-932085-93-8

✧ Contents ✧

✦ Foreword ✦

Companions for the Journey

Just as food is required for human life, so are companions. Indeed, the word *companions* comes from two Latin words: *com,* meaning "with," and *panis,* meaning "bread." Companions nourish our heart, mind, soul, and body. They are also the people with whom we can celebrate the sharing of bread.

Perhaps the most touching stories in the Bible are about companionship: the Last Supper, the wedding feast at Cana, the sharing of the loaves and the fishes, and Jesus' breaking of bread with the disciples on the road to Emmaus. Each incident of companionship with Jesus revealed more about his mercy, love, wisdom, suffering, and hope. When Jesus went to pray in the   Garden of Olives, he craved the companionship of the Apostles. They let him down. But God sent the Spirit to inflame the hearts of the Apostles, and they became faithful companions to Jesus and to each other.

Throughout history, other faithful companions have followed Jesus and the Apostles. These saints and mystics have also taken the journey from conversion, through suffering, to resurrection. Just as they were inspired by the holy people who went before them, so too may you take them as your companions as you walk on your spiritual journey.

The Companions for the Journey series is a response to the spiritual hunger of Christians. This series makes available the rich spiritual teachings of mystics and guides whose wisdom can help us on our pilgrimages. As you complete the last meditation in each volume, it is hoped that you will feel supported, challenged, and affirmed by a soul-companion on your spiritual journey.

The spiritual hunger that has emerged over the last twenty years is a great sign of renewal in Christian life. People fill retreat programs and workshops on topics in spirituality. The demand for spiritual directors exceeds the number available. Interest in the lives and writings of saints and mystics is increasing as people search for models of whole and holy Christian life.

Praying with Clare of Assisi

Praying with Clare of Assisi is more than just a book about Clare's spirituality. This book seeks to engage you in praying in the way that Clare did about issues and themes that were central to her experience. Each meditation can enlighten your understanding of her spirituality and lead you to reflect on your own experience.

The goal of *Praying with Clare of Assisi* is that you will discover Clare's rich spirituality and integrate her spirit and wisdom into your relationship with God, with your brothers and sisters, and with your own heart and mind.

Suggestions for Praying with Clare

Meet Clare of Assisi, a fascinating companion for your pilgrimage, by reading the introduction to this book, which begins on page 13. It provides a brief biography of Clare and an outline of the major themes of her spirituality.

Once you meet Clare, you will be ready to pray with her and to encounter God, your sisters and brothers, and yourself in new and wonderful ways. To help your prayer, here are some suggestions that have been part of the tradition of Christian spirituality:

Create a sacred space. Jesus said, "'When you pray, go to your private room, shut yourself in, and so pray to your [God] who is in that secret place, and your [God] who sees all that is done in secret will reward you'" (Matthew 6:6). Solitary prayer is best done in a place where you can have privacy and silence, both of which can be luxuries in the life of busy people.

If privacy and silence are not possible, create a quiet, safe place within yourself, perhaps while riding to and from work, while sitting in line at the dentist's office, or while waiting for someone. Do the best you can, knowing that a loving God is present everywhere. Whether the meditations in this book are used for solitary prayer or with a group, try to create a prayerful mood with candles, meditative music, an open Bible, or a crucifix.

Open yourself to the power of prayer. Every human experience has a religious dimension. All of life is suffused with God's presence. So remind yourself that God is present as you begin your period of prayer. Do not worry about distractions. If something keeps intruding during your prayer, spend some time talking with God about it. Be flexible because God's Spirit blows where it will.

Prayer can open your mind and widen your vision. Be open to new ways of seeing God, people, and yourself. As you open yourself to the Spirit of God, different emotions are evoked, such as sadness from tender memories, or joy from a celebration recalled. Our emotions are messages from God that can tell us much about our spiritual quest. Also, prayer strengthens our will to act. Through prayer, God can touch our will and empower us to live according to what we know is true.

Finally, many of the meditations in this book will call you to employ your memories, your imagination, and the circumstances of your life as subjects for prayer. The great mystics and saints realized that they had to use all their resources to know God better. Indeed, God speaks to us continually and touches us constantly. We must learn to listen and feel with all the means that God has given us.

Come to prayer with an open mind, heart, and will.

Preview each meditation before beginning. After you have placed yourself in God's presence, spend a few moments previewing the readings and especially the reflection activities. Several reflection activities are given in each meditation because different styles of prayer appeal to different personalities or personal needs. **Note that each meditation has more**

reflection activities than can be done during one prayer period. Therefore, select only one or two reflection activities each time you use a meditation. Do not feel compelled to complete all the reflection activities.

Read meditatively. Each meditation offers you a story about Clare and a reading from her writings. Take your time reading. If a particular phrase touches you, stay with it. Relish its feelings, meanings, and concerns.

Use the reflections. Following the readings is a short reflection in commentary form, which is meant to give perspective to the readings. Then you are offered several ways of meditating on the readings and the theme of the prayer. You may be familiar with the different methods of meditating, but in case you are not, they are described briefly here:

✦ *Repeated short prayer:* One means of focusing your prayer is to use a repeated prayer. It may be a single word or a short phrase taken from the readings or from the Scriptures. For example, the short prayer for meditation 6 in this book is "Come, Holy Spirit." Repeated slowly in harmony with your breathing, the repeated prayer helps you center your heart and mind on one action or attribute of God.

✦ *Lectio divina:* This type of meditation is "divine studying," a concentrated reflection on the word of God or the wisdom of a spiritual writer. Most often in *lectio divina*, you will be invited to read one of the passages several times and then concentrate on one or two sentences, pondering their meaning for you and their effect on you. *Lectio divina* commonly ends with formulation of a resolution.

✦ *Guided meditation:* In this type of meditation, our imagination helps us consider alternative actions and likely consequences. Our imagination helps us experience new ways of seeing God, our neighbors, ourselves, and nature. When Jesus told his followers parables and stories, he engaged their imagination. In this book, you will be invited to follow guided meditations.

One way of doing a guided meditation is to read the scene or story several times, until you know the outline and can recall it when you enter into reflection. Or before your prayer time, you may wish to record the meditation on a tape recorder. If so, remember to allow pauses for reflection between phrases and to speak with a slow, peaceful pace and tone. Then, during prayer, when you have finished the readings and the reflection commentary, you can turn on your recording of the meditation and be led through it. If you find your own voice too distracting, ask a friend to make the tape for you.

✦ *Examen of consciousness:* The reflections often will ask you to examine how God has been speaking to you in your past and present experience—in other words, the reflections will ask you to examine your awareness of God's presence in your life.

✦ *Journal writing:* Writing is a process of discovery. If you write for any length of time, stating honestly what is on your mind and in your heart, you will unearth much about who you are, how you stand with your God, what deep longings reside in your soul, and more. In some reflections, you will be asked to write a dialog with Jesus or someone else. If you have never used writing as a means of meditation, try it. Reserve a special notebook for your journal writing. If desired, you can go back to your entries at a future time for an examen of consciousness.

✦ *Action:* Occasionally, a reflection will suggest singing a favorite hymn, going out for a walk, or undertaking some other physical activity. Actions can be meaningful forms of prayer.

Using the Meditations for Group Prayer

If you wish to use the meditations for community prayer, these suggestions may help:

✦ Read the theme to the group. Call the community into the presence of God, using the short opening prayer. Invite one or two participants to read one or both readings. If you use both readings, observe the pause between them.

✦ The reflection commentary may be used as a reading, or it can be deleted, depending on the needs and interests of the group.

✦ Select one of the reflection activities for your group. Allow sufficient time for your group to reflect, to recite a centering prayer, to accomplish a studying prayer *(lectio divina)*, or to finish an examen of consciousness. Depending on the group and the amount of available time, you may want to invite the participants to share their reflections, responses, or petitions with the group.

✦ Reading the passage from the Scriptures may serve as a summary of the meditation.

✦ If a formulated prayer or a psalm is given as a closing, it may be recited by the entire group. Or you may ask participants to offer their own prayers for the closing.

Now you are ready to begin praying with Clare of Assisi, a faithful and caring companion on this stage of your spiritual journey. It is hoped that you will find her to be a true soul-companion.

CARL KOCH
Editor

✧ Introduction ✧

Clare of Assisi: Breaking New Ground

Noblewomen born during the Middle Ages were allowed few choices about their life. Even though the law permitted them to inherit land, they were expected to marry well and expand the family wealth. Some noblewomen escaped these arranged marriages by joining a religious order, their dowries gaining them admittance into a monastery and an assurance of life-long security. Clare of Assisi broke with convention; she walked away from both marriage and the traditional monastic life.

Under God's guidance, Clare made her own choices and created a new path. She took a vow of virginity, for she wanted only a divine lover. She refused to keep her inheritance of land, for she wanted to live unencumbered. She crossed social boundaries and gave to the lower class what she received from her family. In this act of disinheritance, Clare opened a new path for women.

She renounced her privileged position in the nobility, for she believed that having more than she needed denied food and basic necessities to poor people. She refused to follow the old monastic way, for it spoke to her of wealth and security. Because Clare was not afraid to say no, she was able to be an agent of change in a rigidly stratified, oppressive social system. Clare embraced poverty, humility, and charity as companions for her spiritual journey.

Clare attended to, honored, and acted upon her inner experience. She refused to be defined by culture or the church in traditional roles for women. She held fast to her inner truth despite constant misunderstandings and setbacks. Clare believed in what she did, and she wanted to preserve this new way for women to lead consecrated lives in the church. She was the first woman to incorporate her experience, and that of her sisters, into the formulation of a rule. Clare of Assisi persisted so that her spiritual descendants could live as she had lived, in the spirit of the Gospels.

Clare's Story

Assisi stands on a foothill of Monte Subasio, the tallest of the mountains that rim the Umbrian Valley in the heart of Italy. Throughout the centuries, Assisi breathed the life of the cultural developments of the Eastern and Western worlds because of its central location along the trade routes that crisscrossed Italy. Rocca Maggiore, the fortress atop the foothill, provided a lookout station to warn its citizens of encroaching enemies. The city of Assisi proper lies on the south slope of Monte Subasio, so that it catches the sun and is sheltered from northern storms coming across the Alps.

An ancient Roman town, Assisi was one of the earliest sites of Christianity in Europe. The Cathedral of San Rufino was named after the town's first bishop, who was martyred in the attempt to establish Christianity in the third century. The noble class gathered in the magnificent piazza in upper Assisi. Farther down Assisi's narrow, winding streets, itinerants and the newly-formed merchant class gathered on the Piazza del Commune. Bishop Guido resided on the cathedral grounds of Santa Maria Maggiore, the focal point in the town's life.

At the turn of the twelfth century, with increased trade and prosperity in the hands of merchants, a restiveness stirred among the citizens of Assisi. Many of them, such as Pietro Bernardone, father of Francis of Assisi, had accumulated wealth from trading. They grew discontent because feudal lords held all the power and land. Indeed, this new merchant class was beginning to wedge itself between the nobility and the have-nots, Assisi's *minores*. A bloody civil war ensued that turned the entire social system upside down.

Clare lived in a colorful and bloody era. Towns grew to become centers of European economic, social, and political life. Knights rode forth to the Crusades. The Holy Roman Emperor, Frederick II, dominated Europe and fought with the papacy. Five popes sat on Peter's throne during Clare's life, including the powerful Innocent III and Gregory IX. In various ways, all of these forces influenced Clare.

Clare's Early Life

Few details exist of Clare's early life. Even the date of her birth in 1193 is conjecture. Her father, Favarone, was a count, and sources indicate that he was one of seven great and wealthy knights in the Offreduccio family.

When Clare was a small child, the political situation in Assisi became so dangerous for the women and children of the noble class that they fled to nearby Perugia. The merchant class of Assisi was forcing its way into power, thus crippling the feudal system. New city-states began forming throughout Italy. During the first decade of the thirteenth century, the social order in Assisi stabilized enough for the young Clare to return to the city with her mother and her two sisters.

Although the political circumstances had calmed, a religious ferment was just beginning in Assisi. It started when Francis Bernardone, in his early twenties, denounced his father, Pietro, and his wealth in a dramatic public ceremony on the piazza of Santa Maria Maggiore. Francis declared that he had no father but his Father in heaven.

Some time before this, while Francis was praying before the cross in the little church of San Damiano outside the city walls, he heard the image of Christ on the cross call him by name, saying, "'Francis, go, repair my house, which, as you see, is falling completely to ruin'" (Marion A. Habig, ed., *St. Francis of Assisi, Writings and Early Biographies*, p. 370). Interpreting this literally, Francis enlisted the help of passersby, beseeching them to bring oil for the lamps and stones to repair the walls because one day ladies would dwell there who would glorify the church.

Clare's Radical Commitment to Christ

In the meantime, Clare grew into a beautiful young woman. Years later, Lord Ranieri, a local nobleman, testified that he and many other knights had wished to marry the beautiful Clare. She refused all such proposals. Instead, the fervent young woman counseled Lord Ranieri that he should not be so concerned about the things of this world.

Clare had already made a private vow of virginity because she was determined to dedicate herself to the service of God by remaining in her home, living a life of prayer, and helping those most in need. She also decided to divest herself of her entire inheritance in order to give the money to the poor.

Clare lived as a penitent, secluded within the Offreduccio household, praying together with an extended family of women, including two neighboring sisters, Pacifica and Bona. They were joined by two other noblewomen Clare had known during her exile in Perugia: Philippa di Ghislerio and Benvenuta of Perugia. Like her mother, Ortulana, Clare earned a public reputation throughout all of Assisi for her good works, her virtue, and her holy manner of living.

Then Francis came to see Clare. Perhaps he was looking for a group of holy women to fulfill his prophecy that San Damiano would be a home for a community of women. Beatrice, Clare's sister, believed that Francis came because he heard about Clare's holiness.

Little is known of what happened in their first visit, but subsequently Clare, accompanied by a companion, met frequently with Francis. Perhaps Clare had heard Francis preach in the Cathedral of San Rufino and needed some persuasion to follow in the footsteps of Jesus more closely. Perhaps Francis needed to convince Clare to begin a new way of life with her community.

Whatever happened between Francis and Clare, on Palm Sunday, 1212, Clare took a dramatic, irrevocable step on her spiritual journey. The noblewomen of Assisi, dressed in their finest clothing, paraded through the town to receive the blessed palms at the altar of the cathedral. Clare stood aside from this group. Nevertheless, Bishop Guido came to her and placed a palm in her hand.

Recollecting this act later, many witnesses came to see it as the bishop's approval of Clare's plan, a plan that unfolded later in the day when she slipped through the door of her family home and down the winding streets of Assisi. Clare left the city and made her way through the dark olive groves to the small chapel of the Portiuncula where Francis and the brothers waited. She received the tonsure and the drab garb of the Poor Friars. Then Francis's brothers accompanied Clare to the Monastery of San Paolo in Bastia where she found sanctuary at the consecrated altar of the Benedictines.

A woman of Clare's stature and beauty could not defy the customs of her family and her culture without a dramatic reaction. Clare's Uncle Monaldo came with force to reclaim her, but he withdrew because the Benedictine property was reserved as a sanctuary from violence.

Next, Clare moved to Sant' Angelo in Panzo, a residential area on the side of Monte Subasio. Her sister Agnes joined her. Clare's relatives came again, and this time they attempted to forcibly drag Agnes away. According to legend, they ceased their abuse because of Clare's prayerful intervention. Thus Clare and her sister waited at Sant' Angelo until the little church of San Damiano was sufficiently repaired to receive them.

A Community of Poor Ladies

Even though Clare's renown grew, only the outline of her life is known. She would not have wanted it any other way. Clare chose an enclosed life, an obscure life, and separating historical fact from legend proves inexact. However, what is known is that once Clare and Agnes made their home at San Damiano, women from Assisi and other towns came to join them.

Eventually, Clare's older sister, Beatrice, and her mother, Ortulana, came to live in the community of San Damiano. Pacifica Guelfuccio, who lived on the piazza of San Rufino, and Philippa di Ghislerio and Benvenuta of Perugia, who knew Clare and had prayed with her in the Offreduccio household, also joined them. Lady Cristiana, who had been in Clare's home the night of her flight to the Portiuncula, came to live at San Damiano within a short time.

Beatrice said that her sister's holiness consisted:

> . . . in her virginity, humility, patience, and kindness; in the necessary correction and sweet admonition of her sisters; in the continuous application to her prayer and contemplation, abstinence and fasting; in the roughness of her bed and clothing; in the disregard of herself, the fervor of her love of God, her desire for martyrdom, and, most especially, in her love of the Privilege of Poverty. (Regis J. Armstrong, ed. and trans., *Clare of Assisi: Early Documents*, p. 165)

The women of the Monastery of San Damiano strove to live the Gospels in a way that they had not been lived before. Although the Gospels provided the central focus of their life, the inspiration and example of Francis provided a key influence. In her Testament, Clare recalls how she and a few other sisters promised obedience to Francis for he saw that, although they were weak and frail, they "did not shirk deprivation, poverty, hard work, trial, or the shame and contempt of the world" (*Early Documents*, p. 56). Clare wrote that Francis promised always to "have the same loving care and special solicitude for us as for his own brothers" (p. 56).

Clare, like Francis, wanted to establish a community quite different from those that existed during this era. Most religious houses in Clare's time were filled with noblewomen who brought with them large dowries that helped to sustain the properties of the monastery. Some even brought their servants along so that they could continue to live in the manner to which they were accustomed. Although some abbesses stood as examples of great holiness, many ruled with more managerial astuteness than Christlike charity.

Both Clare and Francis considered all persons to be equal in the sight of God. Although many of Clare's community came from the nobility, they spurned personal wealth and embraced radical simplicity. They ate whatever food the brothers begged for them, wore simple clothing, gardened, and wove cloth. Clare insisted that the sisters at the Monastery of San Damiano sustain themselves through the work of their hands and through alms.

The Poor Ladies rose early, prayed the liturgical hours of the Divine Office, wore woolen clothing, worked in the garden with their hands, ate dried vegetables and legumes, drank water, stopped to pray the hour of None, returned to work, ate more dried food, prayed the evening liturgical hours, and slept on straw mattresses in a large dormitory room. On church feast days, those who needed extra sustenance ate a little dried meat.

The canonical hours divided the monastic day:

Each day in the medieval world was divided according to the Roman method of keeping time. Daylight and darkness were divided into two twelve-hour periods, so that as the times of sunrise until sunset varied day by day with the season of the year, so did the length of the "hours.". . . A winter's day of monastic prayer began at two in the morning at Matins. Lauds was recited at daybreak, followed by Prime at sunrise. Because the shorter daytime offices were held at the first, third, sixth, and ninth hours, they were called Prime, Terce, Sext, and None. Vespers, the evening office, was at dusk while Compline was recited at sunset. (Ingrid J. Peterson, *Clare of Assisi: A Biographical Study*, p. 231)

Accounts from the sisters tell that Clare assumed the most menial tasks, such as washing the straw-filled, vermin-ridden mattresses. The sisters who lived with her said that she never asked them to do anything she would not do herself. She chose the most demanding tasks for herself, and if a sister had a more worn cloak, she would exchange it and use it herself.

The monastery received frequent visitors, and the sisters met at regular intervals about community matters. Because Clare understood that the Poor Ladies shared a common humanity with Jesus, she called them her "sisters," rather than the monastic title of "nuns." At age twenty-one, Clare agreed to accept the role of abbess, but she never used the term. Until she died, at about sixty years of age, she lived among her sisters as one who served.

Contemplation in Action

Clare had a reputation for holiness, even as a laywoman of
Assisi. She was known for her good works, her virtue, and her
spirit of prayer. After she began to live at San Damiano, her
reputation spread throughout the Umbrian valley and beyond. The sisters who lived with Clare and many persons in
need of healing came to her for cures. Parents brought their
children, some traveling long distances. One day, some time
after Clare's mother came to live with the Poor Ladies, a boy
with a film that covered his eye was brought from Perugia.
Amata, another of Clare's relatives, told how this miraculous
cure took place:

> He was brought to Saint Clare who touched the eyes of
> the boy and then made the sign of the cross over him.
> Then she said: "Bring him to my mother, Sister Ortulana
> (who was in the monastery of San Damiano) and let her
> make the sign of the cross over him." After this had been
> done, the young boy was cured, so that Saint Clare said
> her mother had cured him. On the contrary, though, her
> mother said Lady Clare, her daughter, had cured him.
> Thus each one attributed this grace to the other. (*Early
> Documents*, p. 148)

Clare made the sign of the cross over the person who asked to
be healed because she knew that all miraculous power came
from Jesus.

Evidently Clare seldom left her monastery, but her
prayers and those of the Poor Ladies served the entire community. When the armies of the Holy Roman Emperor Frederick II threatened to ravage Assisi, Clare and the Poor Ladies
prayed that the city would be spared. It was. To this day a
citywide celebration on 22 June, called the Festa del Voto, com-
memorates how Clare delivered the city from the Saracens.
When they invaded the cloister, the Saracens came face-to-face
with Clare. She offered herself as a hostage if they would
leave; they turned away without doing any harm.

At another time, the city of Assisi was threatened by
Vitalis d'Aversa and was about to surrender. Sister Francesca

tells the story of how Assisi was spared through the prayers of Clare and the Poor Ladies:

> The Lady called her sisters and said to them: "We have received many benefits from this city and I know we should pray that God will protect it." She therefore said they should come in the morning for some time with her. The sisters came, as directed. . . . When they had come, the Lady made them bring her some ashes. She took all the coverings from her head and made all the sisters do the same. Then, taking the ashes, she placed a large amount on her head, as if she had been newly tonsured; after this she placed them on the heads of the sisters. Next, she directed all of them to go pray in the chapel. So it happened; being broken and defeated, the army left the following morning. From then on the city of Assisi did not have another army over it. (*Early Documents*, p. 157)

Clare's Form of Life

In 1209, Francis received oral approval for his Form of Life for the Friars, which was primarily a compilation of Gospel texts about poverty. However, the Fourth Lateran Council of 1215 decreed that no more religious rules would be established.

Probably because Clare had already accepted Francis's Form of Life, Clare requested and received the Privilege of Poverty, the right to live without communal property, from Pope Innocent III in 1216. In contrast to the great monasteries of the European Middle Ages that held large tracts of land, Clare insisted that the Poor Ladies of San Damiano have neither common property nor individual possessions. But in 1218, as Cardinal Protector, Hugolino issued a new rule for the Monastery of San Damiano that did not include Clare's Privilege of Poverty. He also omitted the rule that ministry to the Poor Ladies be carried out only by Francis and his brothers.

After Francis's death in 1226, a papal bull prohibited the brothers from serving as preachers to the Poor Ladies. In protest, Clare declared that if the sisters were to be deprived of the brothers' preaching, they would refuse to accept the food the brothers obtained for them. Clare's "hunger strike" brought results: Cardinal Hugolino rescinded this aspect of his rule. In 1247, Pope Innocent IV made another effort to write a rule for the Poor Ladies, but again it did not include Clare's Privilege of Poverty. Soon after this, Clare began to write her own Form of Life, which was closer in spirit to that of Francis. This rule finally received approval when Clare lay on her deathbed in 1253.

Clare wanted to live in complete detachment from any property whose cultivation would ensure that she and the sisters would have food. The simple people had no such security, and Clare did not want any either. Church authorities could not understand such radical poverty for a group of women; the Privilege of Poverty as Clare understood it might be all right for men, but not for women. Clare persevered and triumphed.

Clare's Illness and Death

In 1224, the year Francis received the stigmata, Clare suffered a serious illness that forced her to remain bedridden for much of the remainder of her life. At least in part, her broken health testified to the severity of Clare's early penances. In her youth, like Francis, Clare had undertaken many of the popular penitential practices of the era: wearing a hairshirt, giving alms, and fasting. At one point, the sisters became alarmed that Clare's health would be endangered because of her fasts. Eventually, Francis and the Bishop of Assisi convinced her to eat regularly.

Doing penance meant more than repenting of sin and receiving the sacraments; it was a traditional form of religious renewal. It called clerics and religious to the common life, to live according to the Gospels in poverty and charity, to practice virtue, and to work for the common good. Penitential practices also included making pilgrimages, living on alms, and disciplining the body. Clare's contemporaries believed that salvation required a penitential life on earth.

The exact nature of Clare's illness is not known, but she continued to function as abbess of the monastery and to live under her vows. The sisters tell how even in her illness she would work at cloth-making, providing corporals and altar linens to more than fifty churches in the area surrounding Assisi.

Life expectancy in the Middle Ages was short for everyone, but especially for people weakened by a meager diet and hard labor. Clare and her sisters lived like poor people. As a result, Clare lost her health and saw many of the sisters of San Damiano die prematurely. As time passed, most of Clare's intimates passed on before her. She celebrated their resurrection, but still mourned the separation and loss. The death of Francis in 1226 proved particularly painful for Clare. After God, Francis had been her most important consolation and support. She lived twenty-seven more years without her friend.

In 1253, Clare's own death grew close. As had been prophesied in a vision of a Benedictine sister from the Monastery of San Paolo, Pope Innocent IV, accompanied by cardinals from the Roman Curia, came to her bedside to give her the

Eucharist and absolution of her sins. Clare's official biography, The Legend of Saint Clare, tells of her final days:

> When a kind man, Brother Raynaldo, encouraged her to be patient in the long martyrdom of so many illnesses, she responded with a very unrestrained voice: "After I once came to know the grace of my Lord Jesus Christ through his servant Francis, no pain has been bothersome, no penance too severe, no weakness, dearly beloved brother, had been hard.". . .
>
> Finally she turned to her weeping daughters to whom she recalled in a praising way the divine blessings while entrusting them with the poverty of the Lord. She blessed her devoted brothers and sisters and called down the fullest graces of blessings upon the Ladies of the poor monasteries, those in the present and those in the future. . . .
>
> The daughters, distraught at the departure of their kind mother, followed her departure with their tears, knowing they would not see her anymore. They grieved most bitterly since all their comfort was to depart with her and, being left *in the valley of tears* (Ps 83:7), they would no longer be consoled by their mistress. . . .
>
> But the most holy virgin, turning toward herself, silently addressed her soul. "Go without anxiety," she said, "for you have a good escort for your journey. Go," she said, "for He Who created you has made you holy. And, always protecting you as a mother her child, He has loved you with a tender love. May you be blessed, O Lord," she said, "You Who have created my soul." When one of the sisters asked her to whom she was speaking, she replied: "I am speaking to my blessed soul!" That glorious escort was not standing afar off. So turning to another daughter she said: "Do you see, O child, the King of glory Whom I see?"
>
> . . . And, behold, a multitude of virgins in white garments entered, all of whom wore gold garlands on their heads. One more splendid than the others walked among them and from her crown, which at its peak gave the appearance of a latticed thurible, such a splendor came forth that it turned the night within the house into daylight. She moved toward the bed where the spouse of

the Son was reposing and, bending most lovingly over her, gave her a most tender embrace. A mantle of the most remarkable beauty was brought by the virgins and, with all of them working zealously, the body of Clare was covered and the bridal bed was decorated. (*Early Documents*, pp. 228–230)

The news of Clare's death quickly spread through the entire population of Assisi. Everyone proclaimed her a saint. Pope Innocent IV declared that the Office of Virgins should be celebrated, but since Clare's body had not even been buried, the Office of the Dead and the Mass of the Dead were celebrated. Because of the honor given Clare by the citizens of Assisi, her body was carried in a triumphant procession to the little church of San Giorgio where Saint Francis had been buried until his body was relocated to the new basilica built soon after his death.

Clare's Legacy

Clare's Letters, Testament, Rule, and Blessing

The writings of Clare are rich sources of her spirituality. Especially important are the letters written to Agnes of Prague, princess of Bohemia. In 1234, Agnes decided to join a monastery she had built for the Poor Ladies. On the occasion of Agnes's entrance into the monastery along with seven other noblewomen of Prague, Clare wrote a congratulatory letter, urging her to persevere in the way of poverty. On several occasions, Agnes consulted Clare about matters pertaining to the regulation of their life. Clare's responses, called the Letters to Agnes, reveal Clare's convictions about poverty and contemplation. Clare's final letter to Agnes, written in 1253, provides guidance in contemplative prayer through gazing on the San Damiano cross. Although its authenticity is less certain, a letter to Ermentrude of Bruges also expresses Clare's spirit.

In the thirteenth century, following Bernard of Clairvaux's use of the imagery of the spouse as a symbol for union with God, mystical writings by women began to flourish. Clare's letters carry the use of bridal imagery to new depth.

Clare gazed on Christ crucified on the cross and desired to participate in his suffering and death. Union with God for Clare meant union with a God who suffered. Imitation of Jesus included imitating the ineffable charity of the cross. Clare brought maturity to her understanding of what it meant to be espoused to Jesus. Meaning more than the untested love of a bride, it meant surrender to love in a lifelong commitment of untold burdens.

Clare's most personal work is the Testament, a document written during the time she wrote her rule, between 1247–1253. Clare's Testament includes the story of her vocation, written as an exhortation for the sisters to remain faithful to her charism. Clare retells the story of her own conversion to do penance according to the example and teaching of Francis and recalls his prophecy that one day a community of women would glorify God at San Damiano. The Privilege of Poverty is placed within the context of the life of Jesus, "Who was placed poor in the crib, lived poor in the world, and remained naked on the cross" (*Early Documents*, p. 57).

Clare's Rule developed from the Form of Life given to her by Francis, the Privilege of Poverty approved by Pope Innocent III before 1216, the 1219 Rule of Hugolino, and the Rule of Innocent IV issued in 1247. From these, and from her experience, Clare wrote the rule that received approval a few days before her death. Clare's Rule stresses the constancy of divine inspiration, the centrality of the Gospels, and the importance of the friars' ministry to the community. The Rule of Clare also provides for the common life as she envisioned it and the juridical elements necessary for ecclesial approval.

In the last hours of her life, Clare left a Blessing for all her followers, placing them in service to the other members of the church.

The Eyewitness Accounts

Other than her own writings, the most reliable sources about Clare are the eyewitness accounts of those who knew her as a child and lived with her in the Monastery of San Damiano.

Two months after her death, in November 1253, an investigation was held to gather evidence about Clare's holiness and manner of living. Fifteen of the Poor Ladies testified about Clare's life, providing an important primary source called the Process of Canonization. Their testimony and that of five other witnesses was utilized in compiling the Legend of Saint Clare, a document written at the time of Clare's canonization in 1255 and often used today for liturgical readings on her saint's feast day.

Clare's Spirituality

Poverty and the Passion of Christ

Clare modeled her life on the humanity of Jesus. By gazing upon the image of the crucified Christ, Clare came to identify with his poverty, and this became the foundation for her own practice of poverty. Because Jesus was born poor and naked in the crib and died poor and naked on the cross, the only way Clare knew to imitate him was to also be poor.

Clare also understood that being poor was a spiritual condition related to Christ, and that before God she was indeed poor. For Clare, poverty meant emptying the soul to make room for the mystery of God. Thus, Clare commended Agnes, princess of Bohemia, for exchanging material things for spiritual benefits.

For Clare, the Passion of Christ was evidence that temporal suffering is transformed into eternal glory. Urging Agnes to persevere in her commitment to poverty, Clare wrote:

> If you suffer with Him, *you will reign with Him.*
> [If you] weep [with Him], you shall rejoice with Him;
> [If you] *die with Him* on the cross of tribulation,
> you shall possess heavenly mansions *in the splendor of the saints*
> and, *in the Book of Life* your *name* shall be called glorious among men.
>
> (*Early Documents*, p. 42)

Other Key Themes

The Incarnation and the Redemption: Clare's spirituality centers around the two central mysteries of the Christian faith: the Incarnation and the Redemption. As she considered the birth of Jesus and the way the Virgin Mother carried him in the enclosure of her womb, Clare came to the understanding that it is the privilege of each soul to be a dwelling place for God. Thus, Mary the Christ-bearer became her model. When Pope Alexander IV canonized Clare, he called her "the footprint of the Mother of God" because of her belief that each person should give birth to Christ in the soul and because of her many references to the role of the mother in the Redemption (*Early Documents*, p. 189).

Poverty, Humility, and Charity: In imitating Jesus, Clare particularly emphasized imitating the poverty, humility, and charity of Jesus. In order to clothe herself in these virtues, Clare meditated on the cross. Clare considered the crucified Christ as a mirror of the invisible God. By contemplating the crucified Christ and imitating his virtues, Clare sought to become a mirror of Christ.

Jesus' poverty is evident in his birth as he was "placed in a manger and wrapped in swaddling clothes." Jesus' humility is evident in "the untold labors and burdens that He endured for the redemption of the whole human race. . . . Ineffable charity . . . led Him to suffer on the wood of the Cross and to die there the most shameful kind of death" (*Early Documents*, p. 49).

Mirroring Christ in the World: Clare carried the imitation of Jesus to practical terms, urging the Poor Ladies "that they in turn might be a mirror and example to those living in the world" and to each other (*Early Documents*, p. 55). Clare exhorted her sisters to live as examples and mirrors of God, especially for those with whom they lived. In this way, the Reign of God is spread. Clare taught that the bond of holiness stretched far beyond her small community, and she served others by showing a way to God.

Clare for Today

Praying with Clare will help Christians to nurture the life of their soul. Clare gives witness that freeing oneself from acquisitiveness, living simply, and being an empty vessel for God to fill will lead to true peace. She demonstrates that material possessions cannot satisfy our spiritual hunger; despite life's demands, we find meaning in life by exchanging the temporal things for those of eternity. This means putting everything else, as Clare did, after God.

According to both Clare and Francis of Assisi, following in the footsteps of Jesus leads to true life. Praying with Clare before an image of the crucified Christ provides a way to satisfy the restless longing of the heart for God. No love can be greater than that of Jesus who gave his life to make us sisters and brothers in the human family. Clare's example provides a model for Christian conduct: serving others, living in humility, praying regularly with a community, developing spiritual friendship, and extending the healing power of Christ to those in need.

✧ Meditation 1 ✧

Service to Others

Theme: The love of God given in prayer comes to fruition in our caring for and sharing with others.

Opening prayer: God of Compassion, may our hearts be transformed so that we see the poor in our midst and generously share our personal goods.

About Clare

Clare's parents, Ortulana and Favarone, were descendants of the noble class in Assisi. Their ancestry has been traced back to Charlemagne. Although a noblewoman, Clare chose not to take advantage of the privileges of the nobility. Instead of being served, as were the women of her status, Clare served other people, thus serving God. As a young woman, her service took the form of giving money to people in need. In this way she saw herself as a coworker with God.

Clare sold her dowry and part of that of her sister Beatrice in order to aid the needy people of Assisi. Clare even shared food from her own plate with hungry people. When Francis began repairing the Portiuncula, a small chapel in the valley, Clare donated funds. Later this chapel would become the home of the Franciscan Order.

Having founded the monastery at San Damiano and given up her inheritance, Clare, with the other Poor Ladies, lived in radical poverty. They served Assisi primarily through their prayers, which effectively defended the city and protected it from a ransacking by mercenary soldiers of the emperor. Clare wrote to Ermentrude of Bruges, who had begun opening monasteries in Flanders modeled after San Damiano, about the importance of service to people in need: "The *work* you have begun well, *complete* immediately / and *the ministry* you have assumed, / *fulfill* in holy poverty and sincere humility" (*Early Documents*, p. 53).

At the end of her life, Clare summed up her life's aspirations in her instructions for other women who wished to join the Poor Ladies. Her admonition paraphrases Jesus' call to his disciples. Clare states that a candidate "should go and sell all that she has and take care to distribute the proceeds to the poor" (*Early Documents*, p. 63).

Pause: Imagine Clare's thoughts while she was deciding to sell her dowry to give help to the poor people of Assisi.

Clare's Words

Before her death, Clare blessed the sisters of San Damiano, those of the other monasteries, and all who would come after her. In her blessing, she placed herself and her sisters in service to the other members of the church. Whether they served through prayer, as examples of virtuous living, or by direct assistance, they acted as coworkers with God:

> I, Clare, a servant of Christ, a little plant of our most holy Father Francis, a sister and mother of you and the other poor sisters, although unworthy, beg our Lord Jesus Christ through His mercy and the intercession of His most holy Mother Mary and blessed Michael the Archangel and all the holy angels of God, of our blessed father Francis, and all men and women saints, that the heavenly Father give you and confirm for you this most holy blessing *in heaven* and *on earth* (cf. Gen 27:28). On earth, may He multiply

you in . . . grace and . . . virtues among His servants and handmaids of His Church. . . . In heaven, may He exalt you and glorify you among his men and women saints. (*Early Documents*, p. 79)

In a letter to Agnes of Prague, Clare wrote: "And, to use the words of the Apostle himself in their proper sense, I consider you *a co-worker of God* . . . (cf. 1 Cor 3:9; Rm 16:3) and a support of the weak members of His ineffable Body" (*Early Documents*, p. 44).

Reflection

Clare's desire to live as Jesus did was expressed in her great tenderness and concern toward poor people. Clare understood that service to the human family was central to Christ-like living.

In the course of history, numerous people stand out for their works of mercy, and Christian service has always taken diverse forms. Saintly service may include dedicated caring for children, extending hospitality to homeless people, or contributing resources and time for the public good. Like Ortulana, Clare's mother, individuals may focus their service on the human and religious formation of their families, teaching them that they have a unique place in the Reign of God on earth. From Ortulana, Clare learned to devote herself to prayer and charity in her home.

Whatever form our service takes, Clare calls us to be "coworkers of God" among our neighbors.

✧ Recall persons who have assisted your religious or personal formation. Say their names aloud slowly, praying for God's blessings on them. Examine ways in which you could follow their example of mentorship with people in your life.

✧ Pray Clare's words to Agnes, "I consider you my coworker," slowly and repeatedly as if God's voice were saying the same words to you. Talk with God about the service that you perceive is your portion of God's work.

✧ Look around you. What work of God needs to be done? Perform an action in which you have confidence and happiness that you are a coworker of God.

✧ Consider how you might share your material goods today with people in need. Perhaps you can look in your clothes closet and choose to share some items that are still in usable condition. Study any possessions that are in excess of what you need. Plan a way to share these with people who need them.

✧ While Clare was still an adolescent, she sent money to those who were rebuilding the small chapel of Saint Mary of the Portiuncula so that they could buy food. Identify a practical way by which you can help feed those around you who are hungry.

✧ Clare knew that a life of prayer was not a selfish life but a means of service to the world. Listen to the international news today; then pray a litany of places that are in need of God's blessing.

God's Word

Jesus told His followers that when the Messiah comes in glory, together with all the angels, the Messiah will sit on a glorious throne. All the nations will be gathered before the throne, and the Holy One will separate them as a shepherd separates the sheep from the goats. The sheep will be placed on one side and the goats on the other. Then the Holy One will say to the sheep, "Come, you blessed ones, inherit all that has been prepared for you since the foundation of the world. For I was hungry and you gave me food; I was thirsty and you gave me drink; I was a stranger and you made me welcome; naked and you clothed me, sick and you visited me, in prison and you came to see me." (Adapted from Matthew 25:31–37)

Closing prayer: Gracious Jesus, may I develop eyes to see you in all the poor and needy persons that I meet. Give me compassion so that I will give as generously of myself to these people as I would do if you asked me directly.

The Privilege of Poverty

Theme: Clare envisioned poverty as a privilege because it permitted her to give her complete time and energy to the things of God and to identify with Jesus, who was born poor and who died poor on the cross. This kind of poverty must be grounded in prayer: prayer that curbs our desire for possessions and prepares the soul for God.

Opening prayer: Living God, in contemplating the poverty of the Infant Jesus who was born into the world poor and naked, receiving his human flesh from the Virgin Mary, and who died poor and naked on the cross, I desire to live with less anxiety about my possessions and with more generosity in sharing them.

About Clare

The ideal of poverty stirred Clare's heart. Her desire to follow in the footsteps of Jesus motivated her decision to respond to the Gospels in the spirit of Francis and his early companions: "Take nothing for the journey" (Mark 6:8).

The Legend of Saint Clare dramatizes Clare's conviction to embrace the privilege of poverty on that Palm Sunday flight from the Offreduccio household for her investiture:

Since she was not content to leave by way of the usual door, marveling at her strength, she broke open—with her own hands—that other door that is customarily blocked by wood and stone.

And so she ran to Saint Mary of the Portiuncula, leaving behind her home, city, and relatives. There the brothers, who were observing sacred vigils before the little altar of God, received the virgin Clare with torches. There, . . . she gave the world *"a bill of divorce"* (Dt 24:1). There, her hair shorn by the hands of the brothers, she put aside every kind of fine dress. . . .

But after the news reached her relatives, they condemned with a broken heart the deed and proposal of the virgin and, banding together as one, they ran to the place, attempting to obtain what they could not. They employed violent force, poisonous advice, and flattering promises, trying to persuade her to give up such a worthless deed that was unbecoming to her class and without precedence in her family. But, taking hold of the altar cloths, she bared her tonsured head, maintaining that she would in no way be torn from the service of Christ. With the increasing violence of her relatives, her spirit grew and her love—provoked by injuries—provided strength. So, for many days, even though she endured an obstacle in the way of the Lord and her own [relatives] opposed her proposal of holiness, her spirit did not crumble and her fervor did not diminish. Instead, amid words and deeds of hatred, she molded her spirit anew in hope until her relatives, turning back, were quiet. (*Early Documents*, pp. 196–197)

For Clare, voluntary poverty opened the door to growth in God. Freeing herself of the desire for material possessions permitted Clare to attend to God in prayer.

Images of the poor Christ dominate Clare's letters to Agnes, especially the first letter:

Be strengthened in the holy service which You have undertaken out of a burning desire for the Poor Crucified, Who for the sake of all us *took upon Himself* the Passion of the Cross (Heb 12:2), delivered us from the power of the

Prince *of Darkness* (Col 1:13), to whom we were enslaved because of the disobedience of our first parent, and so *reconciled us* to God the Father (2 Cor 5:18). (*Early Documents*, p. 36)

In the same letter, Clare linked redemption and poverty because salvation was accomplished through Jesus' poverty:

The foxes have dens, He says, *and the birds of the air have nests, but the Son of Man,* Christ, *has nowhere to lay His head* (Mt 8:20), *but bowing His head gave up His spirit* (Jn 19:30).
    If so great and good a Lord, then, on coming into the Virgin's womb, chose to appear despised, needy, and *poor* in this world (cf. 2 Cor 8:9), so that the people who were in utter poverty, want and absolute need of heavenly nourishment might become rich in Him by possessing . . . heaven, *be* very *joyful and glad* (cf. Hab 3:18)! (Pp. 36–37)

Pause: Because Jesus chose the way of poverty to accomplish the work of redemption, consider ways in which you might imitate his voluntary poverty as a means of being effective in your life's work.

Clare's Words

Clare wrote sound spiritual advice to Agnes, instructing her that when she would leave the things of the world in exchange for poverty, Agnes would find the tender beauty of God's love. As Clare was writing to Agnes, she burst into a song of praise, a Canticle of Poverty:

When you have loved [Him], You are chaste;
when you have touched [Him], You become more pure;
when you have accepted [Him], You are a virgin.

Whose power is stronger,
Whose generosity more abundant,
Whose appearance more beautiful,
Whose love more tender,
Whose courtesy more gracious.

In Whose embrace You are already caught up;
    Who has adorned Your breast with precious stones
        and has placed priceless pearls on Your ears
and has surrounded You with sparkling gems
        as though blossoms of springtime
        and placed on Your head *a golden crown*
        as a sign of Your holiness. . . .

O blessed poverty,
    who bestows eternal riches
        on those who love and embrace her!
O holy poverty,
    God promises the *kingdom of heaven*
        and, in fact, offers eternal glory
           and a blessed life
        to those who possess and desire you!

O God-centered poverty,
    whom the Lord Jesus Christ
        Who ruled and now rules heaven and earth,
        Who spoke and things were made,
           condescended to embrace before all else!
           (*Early Documents*, pp. 35–36)

Then in summary, Clare proclaims:

What a great and praiseworthy exchange:
    to leave the things of time for those of eternity,
    to choose the things of heaven for the goods of earth,
    to receive the hundred-fold in place of one,
    and *to possess* a blessed eternal *life!*
           (P. 37)

Reflection

For Clare, poverty meant emptying her mind and soul of material concerns in order to fill her heart with the good things of God. Poverty served as her primary way of identifying with Christ, who "made himself poor for our sake" (adapted from 2 Corinthians 8:9). Jesus redeemed the world by taking on human nature. In addition, through the Privilege of Poverty, Clare and the Poor Ladies identified with the lowest strata of medieval society, those who were dependent and without status.

Jesus accomplished the act of redemption not by giving but by being open to receive the goodness of God. Clare's choice to live in poverty translates the action of Jesus for her own time.

> She sought to live a new expression of radical poverty hitherto unknown for medieval women. . . . It appears that she could not be satisfied until she had expressed a more complete abandonment to God in imitation of Our Lord Jesus Christ who hung naked on the cross in complete surrender to His Father. Clare desired to detach herself from everything that might keep her from "running and not tiring" in her pursuit of God's love. (Ramona Miller, *In the Footsteps of Saint Clare: A Pilgrim's Guide Book*, p. 57)

Although she lived in a stable place, Clare insisted that she neither own it nor have a regular source of income. She wanted to live in a state of life similar to that in which the real poor of society lived. This implied that she and the Poor Ladies would be dependent upon the work of their own hands and upon the generosity of others. It even meant that she could be evicted from her monastery since she did not own it. Clare wanted to live like the involuntary poor: needy, powerless, totally dependent on God's providence.

✦ If you have a degree of financial security, think about some ways in which you might simplify your life and share your goods to be in solidarity with people in need. If you are struggling financially, ask God's help through these difficulties.

✦ The virtue of poverty is a disposition of the heart, a detachment from possessions and a keen realization of our complete reliance on God. Consider the things that you possess: To which two things are you most attached? Talk to Jesus about why and how these things possess you.

✦ Consider how advertisers try to convince you that you can satisfy your spiritual hungers by buying things. The next time you desire to purchase an unnecessary item for yourself, purchase instead something for someone in greater need: for instance, food for a food pantry or clothing for clients of a homeless shelter.

✦ Set aside a special day of solitude without human interaction, radio, or television. In the poverty of emptiness, taste the hidden sweetness of God.

✦ Slowly and meditatively pray Clare's Canticle of Poverty. Recollect any times when the blessings of voluntary poverty have become clear to you.

✦ How have your desires shifted over the years? Clare said, "I have what I desire." Do you feel less satisfied with material things and more satisfied with the things of the spirit?

God's Word

Then fixing his eyes on his disciples he said:
> How blessed are you who are poor: the kingdom of God is yours.
> Blessed are you who are hungry now: you shall have your fill.
> Blessed are you who are weeping now: you shall laugh.

"Blessed are you when people hate you, drive you out, abuse you, denounce your name as criminal, on account of the Son of man. Rejoice when that day comes and dance for joy, look!—your reward will be great in heaven." (Luke 6: 20–23)

Closing prayer: May I embrace the paradox that less is more. Loving God, may I realize in my heart and in my actions that the greatest happiness is serving your reign here among my sisters and brothers.

✧ Meditation 3 ✧

Gazing on the San Damiano Cross

Theme: Contemplating the cross of Christ has transforming power.

Opening prayer: Jesus, I stand at the foot of the cross with Mary, John, and Mary Magdalene as witnesses to your redemptive power. Grant me the grace to take up my cross each day to be a source of redemption and liberation in my world.

About Clare

Clare prayed for nearly forty years before the San Damiano cross, the cross from which Christ spoke to Francis, saying, "'Repair my church.'" It presents Christ joyfully resurrected.

Jesus is the visible image of the invisible God. Clare recognized that Christians are invited to mirror the crucified Christ in their own time and place. To do so, Clare taught Agnes of Prague to pray by contemplating the cross so that she could so identify with Christ that she became a mirror image of Jesus:

Gaze upon that mirror each day, O Queen and Spouse of Jesus Christ, and continually study your face within it,

41

that you may adorn yourself within and without with beautiful robes, covered, as is becoming the daughter and most chaste bride of the Most High King, with the flowers and garments of all the virtues. Indeed, blessed poverty, holy humility, and inexpressible charity are reflected in that mirror, as, with the grace of God, you can contemplate them throughout the entire mirror. (*Early Documents*, p. 48)

When Clare prayed before the crucified Christ, she became so united with Jesus that she figuratively became garbed in all of his virtues. The following scene takes place at the end of Clare's life, as she waits for papal approval of her Form of Life and the Privilege of Poverty:

She held the burnished bronze so that the morning light reflected from its surface onto the crucifix that hung above the cot where she lay. She looked into the mirror's center and saw the crucifix. She looked at the crucifix and saw her own reflection. Christ was in the mirror. She was in the crucifix. Crucifix and mirror were both in her. She was herself the mirror. (Murray Bodo, *Clare: A Light in the Garden*, p. 109)

Clare's life imitated both the suffering and the glory of the San Damiano cross, the union of the human and the divine represented in the mystery of the suffering and glorious figure of Christ.

Pause: Focus on an image of the crucified Christ and see your image and images of the persons you love reflected in Jesus on the cross.

Clare's Words

In her second letter to Agnes of Prague, Clare advises:

Gaze upon [Him],
consider [Him],
contemplate [Him],
As you desire to imitate [Him].

If you suffer with Him, *you will reign with Him.*
[If you] weep [with Him], you shall rejoice with Him;
[If you] *die with Him* on the cross of tribulation,
> you shall possess heavenly mansions *in the splendor of
> the saints*
> and, *in the Book of Life* your *name* shall be called
glorious among men. (*Early Documents*, p. 42)

Writing to Agnes four years later, Clare gave specific instructions for the use of the mind, heart, and soul for contemplating Christ crucified:

Place your mind before the mirror of eternity!
> Place your soul *in the brilliance of glory!*
Place your heart *in the figure of the* divine *substance!*
> And *transform* your entire being *into the image*
> of the Godhead Itself through contemplation.

So that you too may feel what His friends feel
> as they taste the *hidden sweetness*
that God . . . has reserved from the beginning
> for those who love. . . . (*Early Documents*, p. 44)

In her final correspondence to Agnes, using the image of the mirror, Clare directed Agnes in the transformation of her own soul through contemplation:

Look at the border of this mirror, that is, the poverty of Him Who was placed in a manger and wrapped in swaddling clothes.
> O marvelous humility!
> > O astonishing poverty!
> The King of angels,
> > the Lord of heaven and earth,
> > is laid in a manger!

Then, at the surface of the mirror, consider the holy humility, the blessed poverty, the untold labors and burdens that He endured for the redemption of the whole human race. Then, in the depth of this same mirror, contemplate the ineffable charity that led Him to suffer on the wood of the Cross. (*Early Documents*, pp. 48–49)

Reflection

The words *contemplate* and *meditate* both mean to ponder with prolonged attention. Traditional wisdom tells us that if we contemplate or meditate upon anything long enough, we begin to identify with and become united to it. This often happens between two people who profoundly love one another. They give each other prolonged, focused attention to the point where they begin to mirror each other's feelings, thoughts, and even actions.

Understanding this principle, Clare taught her sisters to so contemplate Christ crucified that they became his mirror image. As people dress in front of a mirror to see what they look like, Christians should meditate on the mirror of the cross to gradually "clothe" themselves with "the new self, created in true righteousness and holiness" as Paul says (adapted from Ephesians 4:24). In this way, they put on Christ Jesus so that they can be his image for one another.

✦ Place yourself with Clare before a crucifix. Use her words "gaze upon [Him], consider [Him], contemplate [Him]" to move into prayer. Allow yourself to imagine the feelings that Jesus has for you as he gazes upon you.

✦ Look into a mirror and notice the physical changes that have happened over the years. What about spiritual changes? Think of the virtues you see developing in yourself because of an openness to Jesus. What habits of virtue do you still need to "clothe" yourself in to become a "new self" in Christ?

✦ Jesus shared our humanity so that we would know that God is with us. He gave a human face to the almighty and all-loving God. Out of love, he suffered for us and died on the cross. Jesus knew that love always involves sacrifice. How have the demands of love required sacrifice from you? How has your suffering for love helped you to identify more closely with Jesus?

Ask Jesus for the particular graces you need to love your neighbors and for the faith that love does lead to resurrection.

✧ Consider the scenes of suffering, starving, and oppressed people in our world today made common to us through television. Reflect on the anguish of those people. How are these suffering people images of Christ crucified? What response can you make to them?

✧ On his cross, Jesus forgave his tormentors. Forgiveness may be one of the hardest aspects of the "new self" to put on. Consider someone with whom you have difficulty in your relationship. Ask Jesus to grant you the desire and the grace to offer forgiveness to this person. If you can, offer forgiveness in person.

God's Word

If in Christ there is anything that will move you, any incentive in love, . . . I appeal to you, make my joy complete by being of a single mind, one in love. . . . Make your own the mind of Christ Jesus:

> Who, being in the form of God,
> did not count equality with God
> something to be grasped.

> But he emptied himself,
> taking the form of a slave,
> becoming as human beings are;
> and being in every way like a human being,
> he was humbler yet,
> even to accepting death, death on a cross.

> And for this God raised him high.

(Philippians 2:1–9)

Closing prayer: Lifting up my eyes to you, Jesus, fills my heart with gratitude. Transform my fears and anxieties this day into joy so that I might proclaim the good news of your love to others. Make me over into a "new self" patterned on you, God-with-us.

✧　**Meditation 4**　✧

The Strength
of the Eucharist

Theme: Eucharistic prayer strengthens our faith, drives away shadows of doubt, and nourishes our souls.

Opening prayer: "To whom shall we go? You have the message of eternal life" (John 6:68).

About Clare

Clare turned to the Eucharist when she needed divine strength, as in 1249, the year the Saracens invaded the monastery:

> The Spoleto Valley more often *drank of the chalice of wrath* (Rev 14:10) because of that scourge the Church had to endure in various parts of the world under Frederick the Emperor. In it there was a battle array of soldiers and Saracen archers swarming like bees at the imperial command to depopulate its villages and spoil its cities. Once when the fury of the enemy pressed upon Assisi, a city dear to the Lord, and the army was already near its gates, the Saracens, the worst of people, who thirsted for the blood of Christians and attempted imprudently every outrage, rushed upon San Damiano, [entered] the confines of the place and even the enclosure of the virgins.

The hearts of the ladies melted with fear; their voices trembled with it, and they brought their tears to their mother. She, with an undaunted heart, ordered that she be brought, sick as she was, to the door and placed there before the enemy, while the silver pyx enclosed in ivory in which the Body of the Holy of Holies was most devotedly reserved, preceded her.

When she had thoroughly prostrated herself to the Lord in prayer, she said to her Christ with tears [in her eyes]: "Look, my Lord, do you wish to deliver into the hands of pagans your defenseless servants whom You have nourished with Your own love? Lord, I beg You, defend these Your servants whom I am not able to defend at this time." Suddenly a voice from the mercy-seat of new grace, as if of a little child, resounded in her ears: "I will always defend you." "My Lord," she said, "please protect this city which for Your love sustains us." And Christ said to her: "It will suffer afflictions, but will be defended by my protection."

Then the virgin, raising her tear-filled face, comforted the weeping [sisters] saying: "My dear children, I guarantee, you will not suffer any harm. Just have confidence in Christ." Without delay, the subdued boldness of those dogs began immediately to be alarmed. They were driven away by the power of the one who was praying, departing in haste over those walls which they had scaled. (*Early Documents*, pp. 211–212)

Pause: Ask yourself: How much confidence do I have in the words Christ spoke to Clare in her need, "I will always defend you"?

Clare's Words

The Eucharist is the cause and sign of unity. For Clare, the sacred banquet of the Eucharist was a foretaste of the experience of God in the heavenly Jerusalem.

Happy, indeed, is she
>to whom it is given to share in this sacred banquet
>so that she might cling with all her heart
>to Him
>>Whose beauty all the blessed hosts of heaven
>>>unceasingly admire
>>Whose affection excites
>>Whose contemplation refreshes,
>>Whose kindness fulfills,
>>Whose delight replenishes,
>>Whose remembrance delightfully shines,
>>By Whose fragrance the dead are revived,
>>Whose glorious vision will bless
>>>all the citizens of the heavenly Jerusalem:
>>>which, *since it is the splendor of*
>>>*eternal glory,* is
>>>*the brilliance of eternal light*
>>>*and the mirror without blemish.*
>>>>(*Early Documents,* p. 48)

Reflection

Clare's relationship to God was nourished through the Eucharist, the sacraments, and other signs and symbols given by the church. When in greatest danger, Clare received her confidence from the sacrament of the Body of Christ. According to the Legend of Saint Clare, when she received the Eucharist, she "shed burning tears" (*Early Documents,* p. 217).

Clare's work was linked to the Eucharist. Even in her illness, she sat propped up in bed making delicate cloth: "From these she made over fifty sets of corporals, enclosed them in silk or purple covers, and sent them to various churches throughout the plains and mountains of Assisi" (*Early Documents,* p. 217). Clare's life with Christ centered around the Eucharist, in which she tasted the sweetness of the Bread of Life and gained renewed strength for the journey onward.

✧ Slowly reread Clare's Words on sharing in the sacred banquet of eternity. Ponder each phrase and how it relates to your experience of the Eucharist.

✧ Reflect on what you fear the most, and write a list of your fears. The Poor Ladies who were next to Clare at the time of the Saracen invasion heard Christ tell her, "'I will always defend you.'" As you ponder each of your fears, hear Christ reassure you in the same words.

✧ Recall some event in your life that could have been tragic but was not, because of God's strength. Pray for faith to believe that God will continue to care for you in your most desperate needs.

✧ After Assisi was spared from attack by the Saracens through Clare's intercession, the Poor Ladies fasted and ab-stained for a whole day in gratitude. For the next few days,

write a list of the blessings of each day. End the week of blessings with a fast to express your gratitude.

✧ Consider the need of homebound persons to have the
Eucharist brought to them. Inquire about the ministry in your
parish and consider volunteering to be a eucharistic minister
to the sick.

God's Word

"In all truth I tell you,
it was not Moses who gave you the bread from heaven,
it is my Father who gives you the bread from heaven,
the true bread;
for the bread of God
is the bread which comes down from heaven
and gives life to the world."

(John 6:32–33)

Closing prayer:

The angel of Yahweh encamps around those
who revere God and rescues them.
O taste and see that Yahweh is good!
Blessed are those who trust in God.

(Psalm 34:7–8)

Spiritual Friendship

Theme: Intimacy with Jesus strengthens and deepens the friendship between people.

Opening prayer: Jesus, you who called your disciples *friends*, show us the way to true and lasting friendship.

About Clare

After Clare had established the monastery of Poor Ladies at San Damiano, Saint Francis visited when he was in the vicinity and consoled Clare with his advice. She wanted to share a meal with him. He refused several times but, urged by his companions, arranged for Clare to come to the small chapel of the Portiuncula where the brothers lived. The story of their encounter has been recorded in the *Little Flowers of St. Francis:*

> And she came to St. Mary of the Angels. And first she reverently and humbly greeted the Blessed Virgin Mary before her altar, where she had been shorn and received the veil. And then they devoutly showed her around the Place until it was mealtime. Meanwhile St. Francis had the table prepared on the bare ground, as was his custom.
> And when it was time to eat, St. Francis and St. Clare sat down together, and one of his companions with St. Clare's companion, and all his other companions were

grouped around that humble table. But at the first course St. Francis began to speak about God in such a sweet and holy and profound and divine and marvelous way that he himself and St. Clare and her companion and all the others who were at that poor little table were rapt in God by the overabundance of divine grace that descended upon them.

And while they were sitting there, in a rapture, with their eyes and hands raised to Heaven, it seemed to the men of Assisi and Bettona and the entire district that the Church of St. Mary of the Angels and the whole Place were all aflame and that an immense fire was burning over all of them. Consequently the men of Assisi ran down there in great haste to save the Place and put out the fire, as they firmly believed that everything was burning up.

But when they reached the Place, they saw that nothing was on fire. Entering the Place, they found St. Francis with St. Clare and all the companions sitting around that very humble table, rapt in God by contemplation and invested with power from on high. Then they knew for sure that it had been a heavenly and not a material fire that God had miraculously shown them to symbolize the fire of divine love which was burning in the souls of those holy friars and nuns. So they withdrew, with great consolation in their hearts and with holy edification. (Habig, ed., *St. Francis of Assisi*, pp. 1332–1333)

Pause: How has the love of God supported and guided your love of your friends?

Clare's Words

Clare's Testament illustrates the affection the Poor Ladies of San Damiano had for Francis.

Therefore, I, Clare, a handmaid of Christ and of the Poor Sisters of the Monastery of San Damiano—although unworthy—and the little plant of the holy father, consider together with my sisters so lofty a profession and the command of such a father and also the frailty of some others that we feared in ourselves after the passing of our holy father Francis, who was our pillar [of strength] and, after God, our one consolation and support. Time and again we willingly bound ourselves to our Lady, most holy Poverty, that after my death, the sisters, those present and those to come, would never turn away. (*Early Documents*, p. 57)

These passages from Clare's Rule illustrate how mutual affection sprang from being of one heart and mind about following Jesus:

After the Most High Heavenly Father saw fit by His grace to enlighten my heart to do penance according to the example and teaching of our most blessed Father Saint Francis, shortly after his own conversion, I, together with my sisters, willingly promised him obedience.

When the Blessed Father saw we had no fear of poverty, hard work, trial, shame, or contempt of the world, but, instead, regarded such things as great delights, moved by compassion he wrote a form of life for us as follows:

"Because by divine inspiration you have made yourselves daughters and servants of the Most High King, the heavenly Father, and have taken the Holy Spirit as your spouse, choosing to live according to the perfection of the holy Gospel, I resolve and promise for myself and for my brothers to always have that same loving care and solicitude for you as I [have] for them."

As long as he lived he diligently fulfilled this and wished that it always be fulfilled by his brothers.

Shortly before his death he once more wrote his last will for us that we—or those, as well, who would come after us—would never turn aside from the holy poverty we had embraced. He said:

"I, little brother Francis, wish to follow the life and poverty of our most high Lord Jesus Christ and of His holy mother and to persevere in this until the end; and I ask and counsel you, my ladies, to live always in this most holy life and poverty. And keep most careful watch that you never depart from this by reason of the teaching or advice of anyone." (*Early Documents*, pp. 68–69)

Reflection

Clare blessed her sisters, saying, "Always be lovers of your souls and those of all your sisters" (*Early Documents*, p. 79). She valued the way in which friendship provides indispensable nourishment for our love of God and neighbor. At the same time, she knew that love of God gave indispensable nourishment for friendship.

The companionship of Francis and Clare offers wisdom about our own relationships: good friends encourage each other toward holiness. The relationship of Francis and Clare grew in their shared desire to imitate Jesus, especially in his poverty and humility. Their friendship produced great blessings for the entire church:

> The relationship of Francis and Clare should be characterized as a communion of mutual charism and mission. Clare, a woman touched by the Spirit and committed to the path of holiness, found in Francis the perfect guide for the aspirations that had earlier moved her towards a form of evangelical witness. Francis, for his part, found in Clare a leader who could give shape to the hopes of women who sought to share the call to penance and poverty that the friars' preaching announced. Much of the mutual influence that these two leaders and mystics exerted upon one another is found in the writings they have left us. (Margaret Carney, *The First Franciscan Woman: Clare of Assisi and Her Form of Life*, p. 241)

Saints and the rest of us thrive in God's grace; one of the great graces takes the form of friends.

✧ After God, Francis was Clare's greatest consolation and support. Bring to mind the friends in your life who console and support you in doing God's will. Dialog with Jesus about your friends, God's life-giving gift to you. Offer words or a song of thanksgiving for them.

✧ In Clare's Blessing, she cautioned the Poor Ladies always to care for the souls of their sisters. What form does care for the souls—the spiritual life—of your family and friends take in your life? Before God, examine your conscience in this regard.

✧ Clare's Rule encouraged friendship among her sisters, urging them always to "be eager to preserve among themselves the unity of mutual love." If you are in conflict with a friend right now, pray about how you can peacefully resolve the conflict. Then go to your friend, approach him or her with love, and see if you can come to a new bonding of your friendship.

✧ If you have not been in contact with a friend of your soul and heart, reach out to your friend soon with a letter, a phone call, or a personal visit.

God's Word

A kindly turn of speech multiplies a person's friends,
and a courteous way of speaking invites a friendly reply.
A faithful friend is a sure shelter,
whoever finds one has found a rare treasure.
A faithful friend is something beyond price,
there is no measuring the true worth of such a friend.
A faithful friend is a life-saving remedy,
and those who have awesome respect for God
discover such friends in their lives.
(Adapted from Ecclesiasticus 6:5,14–17)

Closing prayer: Grant us the grace, Holy Friend, to handle with care the gift of friendship that has entered into our life by sharing with others what is of utmost importance to us. Bless you, loving God, for friends.

Divine Inspiration

Theme: Listening attentively to the Holy Spirit dwelling within us gives us courage and direction for our life.

Opening prayer: Spirit of Wisdom, influence my thoughts. Spirit of Understanding, enlighten me. Spirit of Counsel, direct my decisions. Spirit of Fortitude, support me in adversity. Spirit of Knowledge, help me overcome ignorance. Spirit of Piety, quicken my fervor. Spirit of Fear, keep me from evil.

About Clare

Clare trusted in divine inspiration in operating the monastery and in ministering to those who came to her. One day, Clare "knew through the Spirit" that Sister Andrea was suffering from boils in her throat and wanted Clare to cure her (*Early Documents*, p. 139).

Lord Hugolino told how Clare had been inspired to direct him to take back his wife whom he had sent to the house of her father and mother for twenty-two years because she had not produced offspring. Although he had been admonished by many religious persons to take her back, he was not persuaded until Clare learned in a vision that Lord Hugolino should receive Lady Giuduzia back immediately and would produce a son by her. While distressed at first, he took her back, and they did have a son from whom they received great joy and consolation.

Clare respected the movement of the Holy Spirit in all members of the community, noting especially that "the Lord frequently reveals what is best to the least [among us]" (*Early Documents*, p. 67). Her rule contains an autobiographical section in which Clare recalls how her heart was moved to conversion through divine inspiration:

> After the Most High Heavenly Father saw fit by His grace to enlighten my heart to do penance according to the example and teaching of our most blessed Father Saint Francis, shortly after his own conversion, I, together with my sisters, willingly promised him obedience. (*Early Documents*, p. 68)

Pause: Ask yourself: If I seek the Spirit's wisdom, do I genuinely trust that the Holy Spirit will guide me?

Clare's Words

In her rule, Clare places the Holy Spirit at the center of prayer:

> Let them rather devote themselves to what they should desire to have above all else: the Spirit of the Lord and His holy manner of working, to pray always . . . with a pure heart, and to have humility, patience in difficulty and infirmity, and to love those who persecute, blame, and accuse us, for the Lord says: *Blessed are those who suffer persecution for the sake of justice, for theirs is the kingdom of heaven* (Mt 5:10). But *whoever perseveres to the end will be saved.* (*Early Documents*, p. 74)

The Holy Spirit was the source of Clare's inspiration for her vocation, for which she daily gave thanks:

> Among the other gifts that we have received and do daily receive from our benefactor, *the Father of Mercies* (2 Cor 1:3), and for which we must express the deepest thanks to the glorious Father of Christ, there is our vocation, for

which, all the more by way of its being more perfect and greater, do we owe the greatest thanks to Him. (*Early Documents*, p. 54)

Reflection

Clare's knowledge about God came from her experience of God's work in the ordinary. Clare had a personal relationship with the Holy Spirit, who inspired her actions. She always attended to divine inspiration, directing each novice, for example, to dispose of her possessions "as the Lord may inspire her" (*Early Documents*, p. 63).

In chapter six of her rule, Clare named divine inspiration as a source of her vocation, pointing out that a sister's vocation is to be lived in relationship with the Father, Son, and Spirit. She trusted in the movement of the Spirit in her heart as the cornerstone of and the highest authority for her life. Following the inspiration of the Spirit at critical moments gave her the courage to cling with tenacity to the way of life she had chosen.

Jesus promised that the Spirit would always be with us, among us, in us. Holy Wisdom dwells among us, if we pay attention to Holy Wisdom's promptings and take them seriously.

✦ Francis used the title "spouse" of the Holy Spirit to describe Clare. How might you describe your own relationship with the Holy Spirit?

✦ In gratitude, Clare attributed her vocation to the Holy Spirit. In one sentence, try to define your mission, calling, or vocation. In order to do this, recall the presence of the Holy Spirit within you. Breathe deeply and slowly. As you inhale, pray "Come, Holy Spirit." Then ask Holy Wisdom, "What am I here to be and do? What is my unique calling?" Meditate on these questions; dialog with the Spirit. When you feel that you can write your mission statement, do so.

Offer prayers of thanksgiving for your special vocation in God's plan. Periodically, review your mission statement; refine it as the Spirit prompts you.

✧ Recall an event in your life when you acted coura-
geously or wisely according to your inner inspirations even
though you had doubts and insecurities. Thank Holy Wisdom
for the courage and wisdom.

✧ Bring to mind some issue that you currently find vex-
ing. Recall the presence of the Holy Spirit. Dialog with the
Spirit about the situation, asking for guidance. Speak to a wise
and helpful friend about the situation. Pray for clarity about
the situation. If clarity comes, rejoice. If vexation remains,
pray for tolerance about the ambiguity.

✧ Have you ever felt a gentle urging to give someone a
call or to write a letter to them, only to find out that the other
person also desired to connect with you? The next time that
someone seems to be on your mind, act upon the inspiration—the gentle presence of the Spirit within—beckoning you
to extend love outward.

God's Word

The Spirit too comes to help us in our weakness. For
when we cannot choose words in order to pray properly,
the Spirit expresses our plea in a way that could never be
put into words, and God who knows everything in our
hearts knows perfectly well what the Spirit means. The
pleas of the saints expressed by the Spirit are according to
the mind of God. (Adapted from Romans 8:26–27)

Closing prayer: Good and gracious God, your word and
the Spirit within me comfort me as I sit in silent prayer not
knowing what to say. You know my heart. You know I love
you. Come, Holy Wisdom, come.

Devotion to the Passion

Theme: Clare believed that the Passion of Christ invites us to consider the immensity of God's love for us.

Opening prayer: Gracious Jesus, we bless you. By your holy cross you have redeemed the world.

About Clare

In his book about Clare, Murray Bodo suggests that Clare saw in Francis an example of the passion of Christ:

> She remembered the first time she saw the poor crucified Christ. She was sitting at the window of her home sewing and absently gazing at the piazza below just as the first rays of the sun were beginning to slide across the cobblestones. She was thinking of the Son of God making his way toward Jerusalem to be handed over to his enemies. She was wondering what Christ looked like as he walked steadfastly toward Jerusalem's gates. Then suddenly, he was there. He wore a tattered peasant's garb with a rope tied around his waist. He was barefoot and unkempt, and children were mocking him and throwing stones at his heels. (*Clare*, p. 83)

Clare's love for the crucified Christ is reflected in her religious imagination and expressed in her writing. In her second letter to Agnes of Prague, she advises her to "embrace the poor Christ. Look upon Him Who became contemptible for you, and follow Him" (*Early Documents*, p. 41).

Clare's devotion to the Passion of Christ became obvious to everyone who knew her. The sisters who lived with Clare testified that she admonished them always to keep the Passion of Christ before their eyes. According to Sister Filippa, "Clare was so caught up in her contemplation that during the day of Good Friday, while thinking about the Passion of the Lord, she was almost insensible throughout that entire day and a large part of the following day" (*Early Documents*, p. 144).

Sister Angeluccia said that once when Clare heard the Easter sequence being sung, she was overjoyed and kept the song in her mind. After night prayer on Easter Sunday, she admonished the community: "My sisters and daughters, you must always remember and recall this blessed water that came from the right side of our Lord Jesus Christ as He hung upon the cross" (*Early Documents*, p. 169).

When Pope Gregory IX wanted Agnes to dilute her practice of poverty by uniting the properties of the monastery and hospice, Clare urged her and the Poor Ladies of Prague to persevere against such an intrusion by uniting herself as a spouse to the suffering of Jesus:

> As someone zealous for the holiest poverty, in a spirit of great humility and the most ardent charity, you have held fast *to the footprints* (1 Pt 2:22) of Him to Whom you have merited to be joined as a Spouse. . . .
> Look upon Him Who became contemptible for you,
>   and follow Him, making yourself contemptible
>   in this world for Him.
> Your Spouse, though *more beautiful than the children of men* (Ps 44:3) became, for your salvation, the lowest of men, was despised, struck, scourged untold times throughout His entire body, and then died amid the suffering of the Cross. (*Early Documents*, pp. 40–42)

In the fourth letter, Clare directed Agnes to pray daily before the image of the crucified Christ so that by meditating upon the Passion of Christ she would "be inflamed more strongly with the fervor of charity" (*Early Documents*, p. 49).

Pause: What objects or practices remind you of the Passion of Christ?

Clare's Words

Look to heaven that invites us, O dearly beloved,
  and *take up the cross* and *follow* Christ
  Who goes before us,
for through Him
  we shall enter into His glory
  after *many* different *trials.*
Love God
  and Jesus, His Son, Who was crucified for us sinners,
  from the depths of your heart,
  and never let the thought of Him leave your mind.
Meditate constantly on the mysteries of the cross
  and the *agonies of His mother standing at the foot*
    of the cross.
Pray and always *be vigilant.*

(*Early Documents,* p. 52)

Reflection

Contemplation of the Passion was at the heart of Clare's life. In the suffering Christ, she discovered God's love for humanity and drew spiritual energy. The San Damiano cross that Clare contemplated depicts suffering as inseparable from the glory that Christ knew. The suffering Christ for whom she wept is the same as the glorious Christ who was the source of her hope.

Devotion to the crucified Christ provides consolation in face of adversity, hope in face of despair, and strength from his example. Clare contemplated Jesus as the redeemer and savior who gave his life to save us. She was overpowered by Jesus' grandeur and his humility, manifested especially through his lowly birth in the crib of Bethlehem. The poverty of the crib and the humility and love of the cross are foremost themes throughout all of Clare's writings.

Since Christ so loves humanity that he became a human being and suffered with us, the crucified Christ becomes the model of the self-giving, generous love that we should bring to our sisters and brothers. In his resurrection, Christ brings the promise of glory for those who keep his commandment to love.

✧ Read the Passion of Christ found in John's Gospel. Ponder passages that seem particularly important for you. Converse with Jesus about the Passion and your feelings about him.

✧ Reflect upon the scene of Mary holding her son after he was taken down from the cross. Pray with Mary about your losses and grief. Ask her to renew your spirit with the hope she must have had in the midst of her sorrow.

✧ Sing a hymn of praise and thanksgiving for the wonder of God's love in sending Jesus, Emmanuel, God-with-us to be your savior, guide, model, and brother.

✧ Make the "Jesus Prayer" your own: "Lord Jesus Christ, Son of God, have mercy on me a sinner." Say this ancient prayer as you drive to work, walk down the street, cook supper, take a drink of water—in other words, at any time when you can attend to Christ directly.

✧ In meditating on the cross, Clare identified with Jesus' sacrificial love. In meditating on the Resurrection, she was consoled by Jesus overcoming death. Fill a bowl with clean water. As you bathe your face and hands, renew your baptismal pledge to live in the footsteps of Jesus, to love your neighbor, and to be reconciled to the people of God. Bless the name of Jesus for the promise of the resurrection.

God's Word

When they came to Jesus, they saw he was already dead, and so instead of breaking his legs one of the soldiers pierced his side with a lance; and immediately there came out blood and water. (John 19:34)

Closing prayer: Clare, you who kept the Passion of Christ on your lips in constant prayer, intercede for us that we might desire to love Christ more.

Healing Power

Theme: Jesus calls all of us to be sources of healing. Christ promises that his disciples will lay hands on the sick, and they will be healed.

Opening prayer: In the spirit of Clare, I desire to grow more confident in Christ's promise that suffering may be healed. Living God, make me an instrument of your healing.

About Clare

Many stories tell how Clare healed needy people by making the sign of the cross over the part of the person's body that needed to be cured. According to Nesta de Robeck, Clare's healing power flowed from the power of the Passion:

> In this love of the Passion the sign of the cross became something life-giving that transported her ever more deeply into the mystery of the love of Christ, and through this sign she received extraordinary graces, especially the power of healing. Celano writes: "The Beloved repaid His lover for her love with outward miraculous signs, for when she signed the sick and infirm with the cross their ills vanished." Sometimes she would touch the sufferer, but more often she made the sign of the cross while praying. "No one ever heard what she said while making the

sacred sign," said Sister Pacifica, "for she always spoke very low." This power was of long standing, for already Francis had sent Brother Stephen to her when he was losing his reason, together with a leper to be thus signed and both were healed. Sister Cecilia was cured of a violent cough; Cristiana of deafness; Amata of dropsy; Benvenuta, who for two years had been voiceless, dreamed on the vigil of the Assumption that Clare would cure her the next day, as indeed happened; another Benvenuta suffered from ulcers for twelve years and she too was cured. On another occasion, five Sisters in the infirmary were all instantaneously cured when Clare made the sign of the cross. There were many other cases, and the sick, and especially lepers, came from all round the countryside, and Clare shared her power of healing with Ortolana. "Go to my Mother, she will help you," and like her daughter, Ortolana would make the sign of the cross and pray, and her fame as a healer was also widespread. (*St. Clare of Assisi*, pp. 92–93)

Pause: Make the sign of the cross over a part of your body that needs healing and ask God's blessing upon your health.

Clare's Words

Clare performed miracles to heal the body, and she also prescribed a way of life at the monastery of diligent care for the sick. In Clare's Rule, she instructs:

Concerning the sick sisters, let the Abbess be strictly bound to inquire diligently, by herself and through other sisters, what their illness requires both by way of counsel as well as food and other necessities. Let her provide for them charitably and kindly according to the resources of the place. [Let this be done] because all are bound to serve and provide for their sisters who are ill just as they would wish to be served themselves if they were suffering from any illness. Let each one confidently manifest her needs to the other. For if a mother loves and nourishes her child according to the flesh, should not a sister love and nourish her sister according to the Spirit even more lovingly? (*Early Documents*, p. 71)

Reflection

Suffering is a universal human experience. It implies disintegration, disease, and woundedness. As a result, human beings cry for healing. God has created humanity with the inherent power to participate in their own healing. Cuts immediately begin to close and cleanse themselves, and the human spirit seeks light and aliveness.

Jesus became incarnate to manifest God's abiding presence and love within and among humanity. He who is love invites us to heal ourselves and one another. Many avenues of healing lay open to us. Among the acts of Christian healing are prayer, medical treatment, and healing touch. We also heal by spreading the truth that sets us free.

For her part, Clare lived the Gospels with such totality that she became identified with the mission of Jesus to heal. Clare seemed to be conscious of the blessings given to her by God and generously communicated those blessings to others. Clare healed through her prayer, but more important, through her actions. With Clare, all who follow Jesus are called to extend his mission to heal. She gave us an example of taking to heart and putting into action Jesus' invitation: "'The kingdom of Heaven is close at hand. Cure the sick, raise the dead, cleanse those suffering from virulent skin-diseases, drive out devils'" (Matthew 10:7–8a).

✧ What relationship in your life needs mending? Knowing it is your mission to repair the breakdowns in society, perform a concrete action to make whole again this fractured relationship. Write a letter, make a phone call, do a favor, or express a word of kindness to someone with whom you have a broken relationship.

✧ When Clare extended healing to Sister Benvenuta, first of all she made the sign of the cross upon herself and then on Benvenuta. She prayed the Lord's Prayer and touched the wounds to administer healing.

Pray the Lord's Prayer slowly and deliberately while imaging yourself administering healing to someone who is sick. Ask God to heal the person you prayed for. If appropriate, visit the suffering person. Just be with them and, if they are open to it, pray with them.

✧ Communal Anointing of the Sick within the parish witnesses to God's ongoing healing presence within us. Inquire when the next anointing service will be and plan to take a family member or a friend to this special worship event.

✧ Read Matthew 8:2–3. This guided meditation may help you imagine yourself as the leper coming to Jesus.

Begin by relaxing each part of your body, starting with your feet and ending with your head and mind. . . . Slowly stretch each part of your body. . . . Then close your eyes and focus on your breathing. . . . Concentrate on the rhythm of breathing in and breathing out until you are breathing deliberately and deeply.

Imagine that you are among the large crowd at the foot of the mountain waiting for Jesus to come down. . . . Look around you and observe what kind of persons are waiting for Jesus. . . . Can you tell by their external appearance what their needs are? . . . Are the people polite or impatient as they wait to ask Jesus to cure their problems? . . . What physical or spiritual ailment do you want Jesus to cure?

Imagine yourself being jostled by the great crowd as you wait. . . . You grow tired, cold, and hungry. You feel out of control. . . . How important is healing for you? . . . Is it worth waiting to have Jesus meet you in his time? . . . What are your other options if you are not healed? . . . What does the rest of the crowd do as time drags on?

Feel the sudden excitement as the leper bursts forward to announce to Jesus, "Sir, if you will to do so, you can cure me." . . . You watch Jesus stretch out his hand, touch the leper, and say, "Of course I want to! Be cured." . . . See his leprosy disappear. . . . What do the crowds do? . . . What do you do?

Imagine stretching to touch Jesus, asking to be cured. . . . Immediately, hear Jesus' reply: "Of course I want to! Be cured." . . . See your suffering eased. . . . How do you feel?

Gradually come back to the present. . . . Be grateful for Jesus' power to heal. . . . Make a renewed act of faith that Jesus desires to heal you.

When you have completed this guided meditation with Jesus and the leper, you may want to write down your reflections about it and your faith in Jesus' desire for your wholeness.

✦ Over and over, pray the words of Jesus, "Be cured."

✧ List ways in which you can bring Jesus' healing into your everyday life. Embrace and honor even small acts of kindness and compassion, remembering the adage:

Plant an act; reap a habit.
Plant a habit; reap a virtue.
Plant a virtue; reap a character.
Plant a character; reap a destiny.

What acts of healing can you plant each day? Pray for the grace you need to be a healer in your world.

God's Word

Jesus told his followers: "Go everywhere and tell everyone the Good News. Those who believe and are baptized will come to salvation. . . . And here are the ways in which you can tell believers. Using my name they will exorcise demons. They will speak in tongues. . . . They will lay hands upon the suffering who will become whole again." (Adapted from Mark 16:15–18)

Closing prayer: Jesus, may I learn from Clare's example to confidently extend my gift of healing to others. Heal me of all that is wounded, but first let me learn compassion from my own suffering.

The Work of Our Hands

Theme: Constructive work should be honored. Our manner of working contributes to our spirit of prayer and devotion.

Opening prayer: Holy Spirit, open my heart to embrace Clare's exhortation on work: "They must do this in such a way that, while they banish idleness, the enemy of the soul, they do not extinguish the Spirit of holy prayer and devotion to which all other things of our earthly existence must contribute" (*Early Documents*, p. 70). As I work, may I steadily remember that you are with me.

About Clare

Some time after Clare moved to San Damiano, Francis gave her community a Form of Life. Because the Monastery of San Damiano did not have property, the Poor Ladies supported themselves by the work of their hands and by alms, thus identifying with the poor people around them. Clare's insistence upon work is linked to her spirit of poverty. The nobility in Clare's society did not labor; to work equaled living poorly.

As Clare recalled in her Testament, the hard work of the Poor Ladies moved Francis to bind himself to them:

When the blessed Francis saw, however, that, although we were physically weak and frail, we did not shirk deprivation, poverty, hard work, trial, or the shame or contempt of the world—rather, we considered them as great delights, as he had frequently examined us according to the example of the saints and his brothers—he greatly rejoiced in the Lord. And moved by compassion for us, he bound himself, both through himself and through his Order, to always have the same loving care and special solicitude for us as for his own brothers. (*Early Documents*, p. 56)

Clare balanced times of work and times of prayer, keeping a rhythm to foster devotion. Sister Cecilia testified how Clare spun cloth to make corporals for the churches around Assisi:

Lady Clare, never wanting to be idle at any time, even during the time of her last illness, made herself rise, sit up in bed and spin. The soft cloth made by her spinning she used to make many corporals and the cases to hold them, covered with silk or precious cloth. She sent them . . . to the churches of the Assisi diocese. (*Early Documents*, p. 152)

Pause: Reflect on this question: How does my work help me identify with other laborers—especially poor ones—in the world?

Clare's Word

Trying to encourage Ermentrude of Bruges, Clare wrote:

The work you have begun well, *complete* immediately
and *the ministry* you have assumed,
fulfill in holy poverty and sincere humility.
Do not be afraid, daughter.
God, Who is *faithful in all* . . . *words*
and holy in all . . . *deeds*,
will pour . . . blessings upon you and your sisters;
and He will be your helper and the best consoler;
He is our redeemer and our eternal reward.
(*Early Documents*, p. 53)

In the seventh chapter of her Form of Life, Clare described a manner of work that does not extinguish the spirit of prayer and devotion.

> Let the sisters to whom the Lord has given the grace of working work faithfully and devotedly after the Hour of Terce at work that pertains to a virtuous life and the common good. They must do this in such a way that, while they banish idleness, the enemy of the soul, they do not extinguish the Spirit of holy prayer and devotion to which all other things of our earthly existence must contribute. (*Early Documents*, p. 70)

Reflection

Because they renounced all ownership of property, Clare and her sisters worked and received alms for support. Their work often was service—service to God and service to one another. Clare envisioned herself as a servant of the sisters in her role as abbess. The Poor Ladies also gave external service to those who came to the Monastery of San Damiano, especially to the sick who sought cures from Clare.

Many of the tasks that Clare and her sisters undertook certainly lacked glamour. However, all work done for the good of humanity can be an act of worship and virtue, especially if we attend to what we are doing. Often we have our minds on some future act, something we like to do better, or some worry. So what we are really doing now gets short shrift and little care. But if we focus on the work we are doing now, we can turn it into prayer. The prayer of the work now at hand precludes our worries or anxiousness about what is next. When we peel carrots, we peel carrots. When we type at the computer, we type, attending to and caring for the work at hand in God's presence.

Work that is constructive cannot be an enemy to the Spirit, if we do it with all the care we can for the glory of God.

✦ Clare served her sisters and those who sought her assistance with tenderness and affection because she knew the tenderness and affection of God's love; she treated others as she perceived God treating her. Clare described God's love as hidden sweetness, kindness, delight, benevolence, and goodness. Meditate on this question: Do I respond to my clients, coworkers, patients, or customers with the same mercy, kindness, and compassion that God shows to me?

✧ Ask Clare for courage not to lose heart and to maintain a spirit of devotion in the face of difficulties you might have at work or, if you lack a job, in being unemployed or looking for work.

✧ As you do some simple, ordinary task today, focus on the work at hand. Give it your undivided attention. As you begin the task—washing dishes, opening your mail, driving to work, whatever—recall that God is with you. Then give your undivided attention to the work. If your mind wanders—and it will—just say (for example): "I am washing dishes before God," repeating this prayer whenever your mind starts to wander. Try this meditative-working for a few minutes each day; then extend the period of time you do it. After a week or two, examine the effects of this work-meditation. Did you do the tasks better? How did you feel afterward? Did you feel closer to God? You may want to expand this simple attention-prayer to other daily tasks.

✧ Can you claim that your work is a cocreation with God's work? If not, can you change your manner of working so that, like Clare, your work provides service to others?

✧ Our homes should be places of nurture, intimacy, and personal growth in mutuality. Homemakers are persons whose main ministry is to make the home such a place. Pray for all homemakers whose anxiety about employment, fear of violence, or debts hinders them from being nurturing caregivers in their home. Extend a compassionate hand to a homemaker today.

✧ Try to list several ways in which you could assist people struggling to make a living for their families. Perform some task to assist those who labor with or who want to labor with their hands.

God's Word

Let love be without any pretense. Avoid what is evil; stick to what is good. In brotherly love let your feelings of deep affection for one another come to expression and regard others as more important than yourself. In the service of the Lord, work not half-heartedly but with conscientious-ness and an eager spirit. Be joyful in hope, persevere in hardship; keep praying regularly. (Romans 12:9–12)

Closing prayer: O loving God, I offer you my work this day in union with the spirit of Clare so that my work and prayer might give you honor and glory.

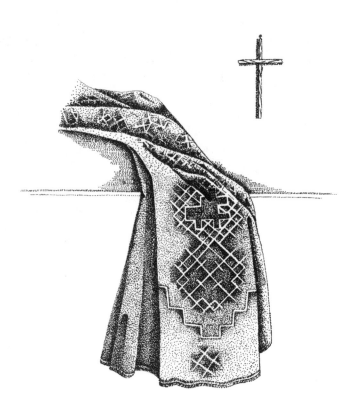

✧ **Meditation 10** ✧

Building Community

Theme: In establishing her community of Poor Ladies, Clare followed the example of Jesus of the Gospels who shows us how to live with one another in harmony.

Opening prayer: God, our creator and font of all goodness, you have loved us so much that you gave us your son to live among us. May we imitate your trinity of divine persons by sharing our lives as a loving family and by helping other members to become all that they can be.

About Clare

In contemplation, Clare experienced the divine dwelling within her, and her love of God united her to her sisters. She respected the divine indwelling in each individual and believed that since the Spirit of God lives in each one, all of her sisters should be loved as she loved God.

Thus, Clare built the foundation of her community of Poor Ladies on mutual charity among the members. Even though she came from a noble family, Clare, imitating the humility of Jesus, did not cling to status. She listened to and valued the wisdom of the youngest member in the group as well as the oldest.

Clare clothed herself in Christ Jesus by imitating his ways. When confronted with critical situations, she tried to imagine Jesus' response and feeling. Clare's actions, like the sacraments, became outward expressions of her burning love of the crucified Christ. Consequently, realizing that Christ loved the Poor Ladies, Clare strove to love them as Jesus would.

One of Clare's sisters, Benvenuta of Perugia, testified to Clare's service and love:

> She was so humble she washed the feet of the sisters. One time, while washing the feet of one of the serving sisters, she bent over, wishing to kiss the feet. The serving sister, pulling her foot away, accidentally hit the mouth of the blessed mother with her foot.
>
> More than this, the blessed Clare used to hand water to the sisters and, at night, covered them from the cold. (*Early Documents*, pp. 134–135)

In this instance, Clare literally followed Christ's example of humble charity to the community.

In Clare's fourth letter to Agnes of Prague, she emphasized the affection that bound her to Agnes and her sisters.

> I beg you to receive my words with kindness and devotion, seeing in them at least the motherly affection that in the fire of charity I daily feel toward you and your daughters, to whom I warmly commend myself and my daughters in Christ. (*Early Documents*, p. 50)

Pause: Identify someone with whom you have a difficult relationship and try to see the spirit of the Lord at work in this person.

Clare's Words

In her Testament, Clare articulates the attitudes that are the basis for building community with others in imitation of Jesus. She exhorts her sisters: "Strive always to imitate the way of holy simplicity, humility and poverty and [to preserve] the integrity of our holy way of living" (*Early Documents*, p. 58).

Clare knew that good example within the community offered encouragement and renewed strength to persevere, so she instructed her sisters:

> Loving one another with the charity of Christ, may the love you have in your hearts be shown outwardly in your deeds so that, compelled by such an example, the sisters may always grow in love of God and in charity for one another. (*Early Documents*, p. 58)

To the elected leader of the community, the abbess, Clare left this directive:

> I also beg that [sister] . . . to exceed the others more by her virtues and holy life than by her office, so that, stimulated by her example, they obey her not so much because of her office as because of love. Let her also be discerning and attentive to her sisters as a good mother is to her daughters, and let her take care especially to provide for them according to the needs of each one out of the alms that the Lord shall give. Let her also be so kind and available that they may safely reveal their needs and confidently have recourse to her at any hour, as they see fit both for themselves and their sisters. (*Early Documents*, pp. 58–59)

By listening to the will of God as revealed through the voices of the members of the community, the abbess offers the direction for the community. Obedience to the articulated vision of the community produces harmonious living. Such obedience comes from a disciplined heart desirous of achieving the plan of God for the entire human family. Clare instructed the Poor Ladies in this manner of living:

> Let the sisters . . . obey their mother of their own free will as they have promised the Lord, so that, seeing the charity, humility and unity they have toward one another, their mother might bear all the burdens of her office more easily, and, through their way of life, what is painful and bitter might be changed into sweetness. (*Early Documents*, p. 59)

Reflection

The ideal that Clare set for her community was that the sisters should live interdependently. Joseph Chinnici describes spiritual interdependence as the primary mode in which Jesus is made incarnate:

> The point is simple: there is something that takes place among people that is at the heart of the evangelical experience of God; the vocation has as much to say about the relationships among men and women, clergy and laity, sisters and brothers, religious and seculars, as about the "religious life" considered in itself. . . . This experience of the evangelical exchange goes way beyond working together, or sharing the apostolate of others, or associating with others in prayer. It cuts much deeper and implies a material and spiritual interdependence where each allows the other to change himself or herself and gives to the others the recognition that the "spirit of the Lord" is at work in their humanity also. In the evangelical experience, this is the primary mode in which Christ is made incarnate; it is a shared experience of the Spirit. ("Francis and Clare: The Vocation of Exchange," *1987 Annual Federation Council Conference: Proceedings*, pp. 7–8)

Clare's Form of Life meant living a common life in unity of mind and heart. Clare's spirituality and her life demonstrate the importance of both mutuality and individuality, so that one enhances the other.

✧ Reread the paragraphs from Clare's Testament that are found in Clare's Words. What meaning does Clare's message have for your family? Your work place? Your parish community?

✧ Clare did not live out the roles other people expected of her; she shunned status. How does her description of the abbess provide direction for your own roles in life?

✧ Think of a time when someone else's action disturbed you and perhaps provoked your anger. If you could relive that moment in the spirit of Clare, how might you respond differently?

✧ Consider persons in your neighborhood who may feel isolated and without regular experiences of community. How might you extend a sense of belonging to them?

✧ List people with whom you are in relationship: family members, friends, coworkers, and so on. Next to each person's name, indicate if your relationship is characterized by interdependence, dependence, or independence. Then, after calling upon the Holy Spirit for light, assess whether you need to make adjustments in these relationships.

God's Word

The night before he died, Jesus prayed: "I do not pray for these only, but also for those who believe in me through their words and example, that they may all be one; even as you, O God, are in me, and I in you, that they also may be one in us, so that the world may believe that you have sent me. The glory which you have given me I have given to them, that they may be one even as we are one, I in them and you in me. May they become perfectly one so that the world may know that you have sent me and have loved them even as you have loved me." (Adapted from John 17:20–23)

Closing prayer: Jesus, wipe away my fears and prejudices and fill my heart with charity. Teach me to love interdependently, to celebrate the gifts of my sisters and brothers, and to build unity in the human family.

The Virtue of Humility

Theme: Jesus did not cling to his divinity but took on the flesh and blood of humanity. His humility inspired Clare to live in the simple truth that all human beings are equally beloved in God's eyes.

Opening prayer: Loving God, by your teaching, may we grow in humility. In this manner the world will know that we are your disciples.

About Clare

Clare was about twenty-one years old and had been living at San Damiano for three years when, at Francis's insistence, she accepted the title of abbess of the Monastery of San Damiano. However, she did not govern with power like the abbesses of great medieval monasteries. Instead, she placed herself in the role of servant to the Poor Ladies. The Legend of Saint Clare details a few of the menial chores she performed for the comfort of her sisters:

> She never shirked any familial chores, to such an extent that she very often washed the hands of the sisters, assisted those who were seated [at table], and waited on those who were eating. Rarely would she give an order; instead

she would do things spontaneously, preferring rather to do things herself than to order her sisters. She herself washed the mattresses of the sick; she herself, with that noble spirit of hers, cleansed them, not running away from their filth nor shrinking from their stench. (*Early Documents*, p. 203)

Pause: Reflect on this question: Do I believe that some acts of loving service are beneath my dignity?

Clare's Words

In imitation of Jesus and Mary, Clare described herself as a servant of the servants. She begins each of her letters to Agnes of Prague by identifying herself as a humble servant of God. For example, in her first letter, she begins, "Clare, an unworthy servant of Jesus Christ and a *useless* servant (cf. Lk 17:10) of the enclosed Ladies of the Monastery of San Damiano . . . (*Early Documents*, p. 34).

Clare's Rule describes the humility that the sisters, and especially the abbess, should nurture in themselves:

The Abbess is to be so familiar with them . . . . For that is the way it should be, that the Abbess be the servant of all the sisters.

Indeed, I admonish and exhort in the Lord Jesus Christ that the sisters be on their guard against all pride, vainglory, envy. . . . Let them be ever zealous to preserve among themselves the unity of mutual love. . . .

. . . Let them devote themselves to what they must desire to have above all else: the Spirit of the Lord and His holy manner of working, to pray always to Him with a pure heart, and to have humility, patience in difficulty and weakness, and to love those who persecute, blame, and accuse us. (Regis J. Armstrong and Ignatius C. Brady, trans., *Francis and Clare: The Complete Works*, pp. 222–223)

Reflection

In *The Spirit of St. Clare,* Heribert Roggen concludes:

> Clare envisioned the role of *servant of the Lord* in an ever more complete way. She did not address herself solely to the community, but really wanted to put forward a way of being in the Church. She considered poverty, humility and service as a task in the Church and a participation in the redemption. (Translated by Paul J. Oligny, p. 34)

Clare followed in the footsteps of Jesus in establishing her place in the monastery as one who serves. By taking on the most odious tasks, Clare demonstrated a disposition of humility.

Humble service extends the virtue of humility from an inner love relationship with God to other people. Humility has little to do with being pious, timid, or fawning. True humility recognizes that God lives in all human beings, that no task done in Jesus' name for the good of a sister or brother is unworthy, and that in God's eyes we are all equally lovable and equally noble.

✧ Slowly reread the About Clare section, focusing on the details given in the Legend of Saint Clare. Then ponder these questions:
✦ Are there services that I consider beneath me?
✦ Do I honestly believe that all people are equally loved by God?
✦ Do I run away from work involving "filth" or "stench?"
✦ What services do I "frequently and reverently" provide to other people?
✦ If I feel degraded while performing menial duties, how do I respond?
✦ How do I treat people whose livelihood depends on performing what society considers as lowly jobs?
Talk to Clare about your answers to these questions and seek her guidance in acquiring the disposition of humility.

✧ Clare described virtues as the flowers that adorn the garment of a holy person. Study how the virtue of humility adorns the robe of your goodness.

✧ How do you feel about having others do something for you? Do you need to be in control all the time? Pray for the gift of humility to receive graciously from others.

✧ Clare's example of humble service is evident in her choice of menial tasks. Ask Clare to help your disposition of heart as you do domestic chores such as cleaning the kitchen, emptying the garbage, changing the oil in your car, cutting the lawn, driving your children to school, and so on.

✧ When Mary assented to being the mother of Christ, she said yes to God even though it would cost her dearly. How are you saying yes to the small acts of humble service that develop into a way of life?

God's Word

Jesus knew that . . . he had come from God and was returning to God, and he got up from table, removed his outer garment and, taking a towel, wrapped it round his waist; he then poured water into a basin and began to wash the disciples' feet and to wipe them with the towel he was wearing. . . .

". . . If I, then, the Lord and Master, have washed your feet, you must wash each other's feet. I have given you an example so that you may copy what I have done to you." (John 13:3–5,14–15)

Closing prayer: Living God, may I always follow in the footsteps of your son, Jesus Christ, who taught us by his holy simplicity, humility, and poverty to serve our brothers and sisters with gladness.

❖ **Meditation 12** ❖

Separation and Loss

Theme: Endurance through times of loss comes from trust in God's consolation.

Opening prayer: Like Clare, I too cry out to God: "'What shall we do? Why do you forsake us in our misery, or to whom do you leave us who are so desolate?'" (Habig, ed., *St. Francis of Assisi*, p. 331).

About Clare

Clare suffered many separations and losses during the course of her life. To follow her calling, she had to leave her home, her mother and father, her noble status, and her entitlements. Her friend and support, Francis, died years before she did. At one point ecclesiastical authorities prevented the ministry of the friars to her community and tried to absolve the Poor Ladies from their Privilege of Poverty.

When Francis died, Clare wanted to view his body before his burial. Since the Poor Ladies lived in an enclosed monastery, the funeral cortege had to pass San Damiano for Clare and the sisters to pay tribute to Francis. When the procession stopped at the monastery, Clare and the Poor Ladies poured out their grief:

The funeral procession up to Assisi was one of triumph with songs and waving olive branches and lighted candles. When it reached San Damiano the Brothers paused and "at the grating through which the handmaids of the Lord were wont to receive the sacred Host, the brothers lifted the sacred body from the bier, and held it in their raised arms in front of the window as long as my Lady Clare and the other sisters wished for their comfort."

Of all people she and her Sisters knew the triumph of their Father, yet, "who would not be moved to tears when even the angels of peace wept so bitterly? . . . Never again shall they have speech with him who will not now return to visit them for his feet are turned into another way! Therefore with sobs and groans and tears they would not be checked in gazing on him and crying, 'O Father why hast thou abandoned us and left us desolate? Couldst thou not have allowed us to go daily before thee to where thou now art? All our joy is gone with thee. Who will comfort us in our poverty of this world's goods, and above all in our poverty of spiritual merits.'" (De Robeck, *St. Clare*, p. 75)

When Clare's sister Agnes left San Damiano to become abbess of the Monastery of Monticello near Florence, Clare suffered unbearable pain of separation. Agnes had been able to persevere in her vocation through the miraculous intercession of Clare, and they intended to spend their lives together at San Damiano. However, Agnes was needed in Florence. She did not return until a few days before Clare's death; they were separated for the greater part of their lives. There is no record of Clare's correspondence to her sister, but this letter of Agnes to Clare demonstrates the anguish of their separation:

> You should know, Mother, that my soul and body suffer great distress and immense sadness, that I am burdened and tormented beyond measure and am almost incapable of speaking, because I have been physically separated from you and my other sisters with whom I had hoped to live and die in this world. This distress has a beginning, but it knows no end. It never seems to diminish; it always

gets worse. It came to me recently, but it tends to ease off very little. It is always with me and never wants to leave me. I believed that our life and death would be one, just as our manner of life in heaven would be one, and that we who have one and the same flesh and blood would be buried in the same grave. But I see that I have been deceived. I have been restrained; I have been abandoned; I have been afflicted on every side. (*Early Documents*, pp. 105–106)

Pause: Consider the good that God has done through some of the difficult separations or losses in your life.

Clare's Words

Piecing together fragments of Clare's writings and stories about her, Murray Bodo pictures how Clare must have coped with her losses:

> She wondered how those who didn't know the Lord survived separation from their loved ones or for that matter, how they survived any tragedy at all. And she was grateful once again for faith, for that gift which sustains the heart and gives meaning to the sometime puzzle which is life.
>
> Clare knew she had done nothing to deserve the faith she now had, and she felt an enormous sadness for those who were without it. As difficult as God seemed at times, at least she knew God existed and that God cared. Without God she could never persevere. It was difficult even to imagine life without faith in a living God who loved her and cared about her. And so she continued to put everything into God's hands.
>
> It was the letting-go that had been hardest to give to the Lord. Letting go of her parents, letting Francis and the brothers move away while she and the Poor Ladies remained at San Damiano. Yet she knew that was the only way—the denying, the love that doesn't cling, the heart made pure by giving away, the sharing. And once she had

let it go, everything seemed closer to her than ever. It was like that with the Lord. You struggled and wrestled with God for something and when you finally gave in and let go, God gave you freely what you had tried to wrest. . . .

That was the hardest test of all: to sit back and wait for God to effect what you would like to take into your own hands and accomplish through your own initiative. But Clare knew that nothing could be accomplished by human effort alone; only the grace of God made anything possible. And so you learned to surrender to God, you learned to acknowledge your own helplessness, you learned that you could not control or be on top of everything in your life.

And once you learned that terrible lesson, everything made more sense. It was easier to let go, to trust, to believe that God would do more for you than you could do for yourself. (*Clare*, pp. 63–64)

In her Testament, Clare admonished her sisters to persevere in their calling and faith despite life's many losses:

Let us be very careful, therefore, that, if we have set out on the path of the Lord, we do not at any time turn away from it through our own fault or negligence or ignorance, nor that we offend so great a Lord and His Virgin Mother, and our blessed father Francis, the Church Triumphant and even the Church Militant. For it is written, "*Those who turn away from your commands are cursed*" (Ps 118:21).

For this reason I *bend my knee to the Father of our Lord Jesus Christ* (cf. Eph 3:14) that, through the supporting merits of the glorious and holy Virgin Mary, His Mother, and of our most blessed father Francis and all the saints, the Lord Himself, Who has given a good beginning, will also give the increase and *final perseverance* (cf. 2 Cor 8:6,11). (*Early Documents*, p. 59)

Reflection

Just because Clare possessed a firm faith did not mean that she was free from grief over her losses. Grieving over the death of

Francis and the separation from Agnes are signs of her tremendous love for them. Even Jesus shed tears of grief over the death of his friend Lazarus. People who love, grieve. Jesus and Clare experienced all the pain and sorrow that we feel when a loved one dies or moves away. Grieving, after all, is part of being fully human.

As in all healthy grieving, first Clare admitted her grief and expressed her feelings. She "wept so bitterly. . . . With sobs and groans and tears they would not be checked." Then Clare's faith permitted her to let go of the grief. She knew that death would not have the final word. Through prayer, she found the grace of perseverance.

Clare provides an excellent example of healthy, faith-filled grieving. First, before God, we admit our loss. Then, we express openly the many feelings that emerge. Finally, after sorting through what may be preventing us from letting go, we do let go: sometimes in ritual, sometimes in solitary prayer, or sometimes in a cathartic talk with a friend.

✧ Is there someone or something about which you have not grieved? If so, bring this person or situation to mind. Ponder all the details of the loss. When you can, express whatever feelings are called forth from this loss. Then, as you are able, ask yourself: Is there anything that prevents me from letting go of this loss? Finally, through a ritual, in prayer, or in a conversation, let go of the lost person or thing.

Grieving may take months to fully complete. The deeper the love and attachment, the longer grieving will take.

✧ Identify those significant relationships that you have lost through ways other then death. Go back in your life as far as you can remember. Remember each person: how you met, what attracted you to each other, things you did together, the best and worst times of your relationship, and the ending.

If a particular loss stirs strong feelings, spend time with the loss. Express your feelings. If you feel like crying, cry. You may find it helpful to express the feelings to a caring, nonjudgmental friend. When you feel ready and able to let go of some of the emotion, a prayer like this may help: "O God, I release my feelings into your hands. Please help me with . . ."

✧ Relax and breathe deeply. Ask the Holy Spirit to be with you in your reflection. Allow any grief still present in your heart over the death of a loved one to come to the surface; do not push it away. Name the person whose death provokes your grief. Invite memories of the life of this person; recall the good times and the bad. Be aware of any emotions that surface with these memories. Reverence the loved one by releasing your feelings. Then ask the Holy Spirit to breathe comfort into your heart.

✧ Pray especially for widows and widowers who are struggling with new responsibilities in life and who need the support of the Christian community. If possible, extend any help that you can to widows and widowers in your community.

✧ Call to mind any losses in your life that you have never thought about before. Identify at least one loss that was necessary before something else that you wanted could come into your life. Talk with God about this loss and the finding of the new opportunity.

✧ Find a comfortable position and prepare to meditate on the losses you have endured. Close your eyes. Relax your limbs and your body. Breathe slowly and deeply.

Imagine that you are one of the people who comes to the Monastery of San Damiano in order to receive consolation from Clare. You are an adult living in the countryside near Assisi and you have heard that Clare has performed miraculous healings. You do not seek a cure for your body, but for the loss you feel in your soul. . . . Do you believe it is possible for you to regain your wholeness through Clare and with the help of God?

As you come close to the monastery you can hear the Poor Ladies singing the Office of the Passion written by Francis. . . . Listen to them as they recite together the invitation of Christ crucified, "All you who pass this way, look and see if there is any suffering like my suffering" (adapted from Lamentations 1:12). . . . Picture Christ, suspended on the wood of the cross, and hear him urge all those who pass by to consider his words.

How do you respond to Christ's invitation to consider his suffering and the loss of his life? . . . Do you back away from his pain and move on? . . . Do you offer words of consolation? . . . Do you attempt to relieve his misery by offering to perform some act of comfort?

You listen and continue to ponder outside the entrance of the monastery until the Poor Ladies have completed their prayers. . . . You knock loudly on the heavy wooden door. . . . A serving sister gently inquires what you want. . . . Tell her what you know about Clare's power to heal that brings you to San Damiano.

The Poor Lady invites you into the visitor's parlor, and in a moment, Clare appears in the room and greets you warmly. . . . How do you respond? . . . She, too, asks why you have come to see her. . . . Pour out your heart to her and explain the loss you are bearing. . . . Take your time.

Ask Clare how she endured so many losses. . . . Ask her to help you deal with your feelings of desolation or abandonment.

Now listen to her words of consolation. . . . Clare wants you to be joyful again and to feel whole.

Ask her to help you understand how the suffering of Christ can console you in your suffering. . . . Ask her what prayers of comfort you can pray that will help to restore your life and spirit.

When you are ready, open your eyes and thank Clare. . . . From time to time, when you feel sad, try to recall your experience with Clare.

God's Word

So then, now that we have been justified by faith, we are at peace with God through our Lord Jesus Christ; it is through him, by faith, that we have been admitted into God's favour in which we are living, and look forward exultantly to God's glory. Not only that; let us exult, too, in our hardships, understanding that hardship develops perseverance, and perseverance develops a tested character, something that gives us hope, and a hope which will not let us down, because the love of God has been poured into our hearts by the Holy Spirit which has been given to us. (Romans 5:1–5)

Closing prayer: Christ crucified, may I grow in love, knowing full well that loss of loved ones brings grieving. I pray not to be spared from my losses but to know the strength of Clare's faith so that I might endure them with hope.

The Centrality of Prayer

Theme: Clare realized that both communal and solitary prayer were essential to growing in our love for God.

Opening prayer: Jesus, I want to always remember your words: "'For where two or three meet in my name, I am there among them'" (Matthew 18:20). Teach me to pray with faith, hope, and love.

About Clare

The life of the Poor Ladies was woven together by common prayer. The ebb and flow between private prayer and communal prayer was established around the liturgy of the hours. Sister Benvenuta describes Clare's enthusiasm for the Divine Office:

> Saint Clare was very assiduous, day and night, in prayer. At about midnight she woke the sisters with certain signs in silence to praise God. She lit the lamps in the church and frequently rang the bell for Matins. Those sisters who did not rise at the sound of the bell she called with her signs. (*Early Documents*, p. 136)

Clare's mystical prayer cannot be separated from her communal experience of the liturgy of the hours and the Eucharist. The sacraments and the signs of the church such as ashes as a sign of penance, the tonsure as a sign of consecration, and the sign of the cross, nourished her relationship with God. Clare and the Poor Ladies of San Damiano incorporated these signs into their community worship.

Sister Agnes testified that Clare would remain a very long time after Compline in "an abundance of tears" (*Early Documents*, p. 159). Sister Angeluccia said that the same thing happened "in the morning at about the hours of Terce" (p. 168). The passionate love that Clare had for her Christ moved her to prolonged periods of contemplation.

The enclosed life of the Poor Ladies preserved the necessary prayerful atmosphere to sustain the contemplative life. The power of their prayer served to renew the Church: "Innumerable cities were enriched with monasteries, / even fields and mountains were beautified with the structure of this / celestial building" (*Early Documents*, p. 201).

Pause: How would you evaluate your commitment to both private and communal prayer?

Clare's Words

When the Saracens threatened Assisi, Clare turned to prayer. When she urged the sisters to imitate Christ, she told them to meditate and pray in front of a crucifix. In short, Clare realized that strength, light, hope, and love sprang from a relationship with Christ fostered by prayer. To this effect she wrote Ermentrude of Bruges:

> O dearest one, look up to heaven, which calls us on, and take up the Cross and follow Christ Who has gone before us. . . . Never let the thought of Him leave your mind but meditate constantly on the mysteries of the Cross and the anguish of His mother as she stood beneath the Cross.
>
> Pray and watch at all times! . . . He will be your help and best comforter for He is our Redeemer and our eternal reward.
>
> Let us pray to God together for each other for, by sharing each other's burden of charity in this way, we

shall easily fulfill the law of Christ. (*Complete Works*, p. 208)

Praying was essential, but how the sisters prayed varied with their ability. Clare's Rule directed the sisters to "celebrate the Divine Office according to the custom of the Friars Minor" (*Complete Works*, p. 214). However, many women of Clare's time could not read, so she says, "Those who do not know how to read shall say twenty-four Our Father's for Matins; five for Lauds;" and so on for each hour of the office (p. 214). Clare was a realist about prayer. Not everyone would pray in the same way, but pray they must.

Reflection

The life of prayer held a predominant place for Clare and the Poor Ladies. Clare's prayer manifested her faith and her love of God. Even during her long illness, Clare prayed assiduously. Clare's sister Beatrice said that Clare's holiness consisted of "the continuous application to her prayer and contemplation" (*Early Documents*, p. 165).

Sister Benvenuta of Lady Diambre said that Clare "taught her to love God above all else; secondly, taught her to totally and frequently confess her sins; thirdly, instructed her to always have the Lord's passion in her memory" (*Early Documents*, p. 162). In other words, Clare prayed in the age-old ways of praise, thanksgiving, petition, and contrition. In addition, she meditated in the silence of her heart.

Prayer had visible consequences. Stopping the pillage of Assisi was one effect. Perhaps more important, Christ's grace poured out in prayer transformed Clare and the Poor Ladies into women of Christlike charity and hope. Prayer has the power to transform us too. An old adage says: Prayer does not change things. Prayer changes people, and people change things.

✧ Faith comes from hearing the word of God and then living it. Read the Scriptures with a friend. Talk about their meaning in your lives and pray together to live the Gospels.

✧ Recall a time in your experience when you came to a clearer vision of truth during a time of communal worship. What was the occasion? Did you ever share this moment with anyone? Why or why not? Make a point to talk with someone about what communal worship means to you.

✧ Sunday has been traditionally set aside for spiritual renewal. Examine your use of Sunday as a day for worship and spiritual renewal. Talk with Jesus about your Sundays; listen to what he says.

✧ Offer God your prayers of thanksgiving, petition, praise, and contrition about today. Ask God for the grace to pray each day.

✦ Saint Paul told the Thessalonians to "pray constantly" (1 Thessalonians 5:17). Most holy people took this admonition seriously. Compose a phrase that has meaning for you, and begin praying it when you wake, and as you shower, eat, walk, exercise, work—constantly. You might pray simply: "Brother Jesus," or "Come, Holy Spirit," or "God of Love, be present now." Try to weave this prayer into the fabric of each day.

✦ Sing a favorite hymn in celebration of God's many graces.

God's Word

Let the Word of Christ, in all its richness, find a home with you. Teach each other, and advise each other, in all wisdom. With gratitude in your hearts sing psalms and hymns and inspired songs to God; and whatever you say or do, let it be in the name of . . . Jesus, in thanksgiving to God. (Colossians 3:16–17)

Closing prayer: Jesus, my heart overflows with joy when I join my voice with others to give praise and thanks to you. Call me to prayer so that I may become closer to you.

✧ Meditation 14 ✧

The Church

Theme: Participation in the life of the church and transformation of the church bring about wholeness for all the members.

Opening prayer: Holy Friend, in the spirit of Clare, I desire to grow in reverence for the entire church, your people and the Body of Christ.

About Clare

Loyal to the church, Clare confronted ecclesial authorities with firmness and conviction. Neither aggressive nor disobedient, she pushed the boundaries of the church to include her vision for women. The Legend of Saint Clare demonstrates Clare's confidence in following her inner truth:

> She asked a privilege of poverty of Innocent III of happy memory, desiring that her Order be known by the title of poverty. This magnificent man, congratulating such great fervor in the virgin, spoke of the uniqueness of her proposal since such a privilege had never been made by the Apostolic See. The Pope himself with great joy wrote with his own hand the first draft of the privilege [that was] sought after, so that an unusual favor might smile upon an unusual request.

Pope Gregory of happy memory, a man as very worthy of the papal throne as he was venerable in his deeds, loved this holy woman intensely with a fatherly affection. When he was [attempting to] persuade her that, because of the events of the times and the dangers of the world, she should consent to have some possessions which he himself willingly offered, she resisted with a very strong spirit and would in no way acquiesce. To this the Pope replied: "If you fear for your vow, We absolve you from it." "Holy Father," she said, "I will never in any way wish to be absolved from the following of Christ." (*Early Documents*, p. 205)

In being obedient to the Spirit of God within her soul, Clare was obedient to the church and enriched it with a new foundation.

In his *Second Life of Francis*, Thomas of Celano articulated the role of Saint Clare in renewing the church:

> It would not be proper to pass over
> the memory *of the spiritual edifice,*
> a much nobler edifice than that earthly building,
> which Francis,
> *under the guidance of the Holy Spirit,*
> founded in that place
> after he had repaired that material building.
>
> It should not be thought
> that it was to repair a church
> that would perish and was falling down
> that Christ spoke to him from the wood of the cross
> in a manner so stupendous
> that *it filled* those who heard of it *with fear* and sorrow.
>
> But,
> *as the Holy Spirit had once foretold,*
> the order of the holy virgins was established there,
> which,
> like a polished mass of *living stones,*
> was one day to be brought there
> for the restoration of a heavenly house.
> (*Early Documents*, p. 268–269)

Pause: Pray for the constant transformation of the church to reflect Jesus Christ more perfectly.

Clare's Words

When Rome refused the Privilege of Poverty to the Poor Ladies of Prague, Agnes wrote Clare asking for her advice and encouragement. Clare responded:

> What you hold, may you [always] hold,
> What you do, may you [always] do and never abandon.
>> But with swift pace, light step,
>> unswerving feet,
>> so that even your steps stir up no dust,
>> may you go forward
>> securely, joyfully, swiftly,
>> on the path of prudent happiness,
>> not believing anything
>> not agreeing with anything
>>> that would dissuade you from this resolution
>>> or that would place a stumbling block for you
>>> on the way,
>> so that you may offer *your vows to the Most High*
>>> in the pursuit of that perfection
>>>> to which the Spirit of the Lord
>>>> has called you.
>>>>> (*Early Documents*, pp. 40–41)

While Clare urged Agnes to hold fast to her determination, she did not encourage disobedience. Indeed, in a letter to Ermentrude of Bruges, Clare instructed her to be faithful to the church despite obstacles:

> Be faithful, dearly beloved, till death
>> to Him to Whom you have promised yourself
>> for *you shall be crowned* by Him with the garland *of life.*
> Our *labor* here is brief,
>> the *reward* eternal;
>> may the excitements *of the world,*
>> *fleeing like a shadow,*
>> not disturb you.

May the false delights of the deceptive world
    not deceive you.
Close your ears to the whisperings of hell
    and bravely oppose its onslaughts.
Gladly endure whatever goes against you
    and do not let your good fortunes lift you up:
       for these things destroy faith and those demand it.
Offer faithfully what *you have vowed to God*
    and He shall reward you.

                           (*Early Documents,* pp. 51–52)

In the first chapter of her rule, Clare pledges her own fidelity to the church: "Clare . . . promises obedience and reverence to . . . the Roman Church" (*Early Documents,* p. 62). She ends the rule in much the same way:

> Let the sisters be strictly bound . . . that always submissive and subject at the feet of that holy Church, and steadfast in the Catholic faith, we may always observe the poverty and humility of our Lord Jesus Christ and of His most holy Mother and the Holy Gospel we have firmly promised. Amen. (P. 76)

Reflection

Clare and her community wanted to bear witness to the church as the presence of Christ on earth. Clare dedicated her life's energies to a life of poverty in response to the poverty of Christ, in the spirit of Francis, and for the good of the entire church. She intuitively understood that unity within the church meant that all members were to live their call to strive for holiness in order that the entire church be rebuilt.

Three times in the Testament, Clare refers to Francis' prophecy that described the Poor Ladies as a community of women who, by their way of life, would glorify the church. Clare remarks:

> For the Lord . . . has placed us not only as a form for others in being an example and mirror, but even for our sisters whom the Lord has called to our way of life as

well, that they in turn might be a mirror and example to those living in the world. Since the Lord has called us to such great things that those who are to be a mirror and example to others may be reflected in us, we are greatly bound to bless and praise God and be all the more strengthened to do good in the Lord. . . .

. . . And loving one another with the charity of Christ, may the love you have in your hearts be shown outwardly in your deeds so that, compelled by such an example, the sisters may always grow in love of God and in charity for one another. (*Early Documents*, pp. 55, 58)

Christ invites all Christians to build the church by being examples to one another of faith, hope, and charity. Sometimes fidelity means challenging the church to return to Christ's simplicity, honesty, trust, and charity, like Francis and Clare did.

✧ Are you aware that your own holiness is a measure of the holiness of the church? What can you do this day to strengthen the holiness of the church? Converse with Christ about the grace you need to build the church through your own example.

✧ Reflect on a time when you experienced obedience to the church that is rooted in listening to a "sense of the faithful." How does this experience help you to understand the meaning of church?

✧ As a medieval woman, Clare was in creative tension and conflict with church authorities, yet she was herself obedient to the spirit of God, the soul of the church. If you feel stress with the church on any matter, first reflect on her advice to Agnes and Ermentrude in Clare's Word. Then dialogue with Clare to seek her advice for an appropriate response.

✧ When the parts of the church are strong, all members gain strength. What gifts do you have that can be shared with the parish community to strengthen the body of the whole church?

✧ How can you work with your congregation in order to promote ecumenical prayer in your local community?

✧ Consider religious leaders such as good pastors, prophetic voices, and inspirational preachers who are striving to make a difference in our society. Which of these persons most inspire you? Write letters of appreciation to them; tell them how much they help raise your spiritual consciousness of the church in society.

God's Word

If we live by the truth and in love, we shall grow completely into Christ, who is the head by whom the whole Body is fitted and joined together, every joint adding its own strength, for each individual part to work according to its function. So the body grows until it has built itself up in love. (Ephesians 4:15–16)

Closing prayer: Pray this prayer, which was offered by Pope John Paul II at the prayer assembly of representatives of all religions held in Assisi on 27 October 1986:

Francis and Clare are examples of peace: with God, with themselves, with all men and women in this world.

Would that this holy man and this holy woman inspire all men and women of today to have the same strength of character and love for God and for all people to continue on that path which we should all walk together.

Moved by the example of St. Francis and St. Clare, true disciples of Christ, and convinced by the experiences of this day which we have lived together, may we undertake to reexamine our conscience, to listen more carefully to its voice, to rid our minds of all prejudice, hatred, unfriendliness, jealousy and envy. Let us seek to be workers for peace in thought and action, with mind and heart turned toward the unity of the human family. And we invite all our brothers and sisters to listen, so that they may act likewise. (John Vaughn, et al., "St. Clare: The Eight Hundredth Anniversary of Her Death," *Greyfriars Review* 6, no. 2, 1992, pp. 186–187)

The Footprint of Mary

Theme: As Mary's womb was the enclosure for Jesus, so we are the dwelling place of God.

Opening prayer: Gracious God, may I be a "dwelling place and throne" for you.

About Clare

The preface to the Legend of Saint Clare identifies Clare as "the footprint of the Mother of God, a new leader of women" (*Early Documents*, p. 189). Indeed, Clare frequently spoke of Mary's role in salvation of the world through Christ. For Clare, Mary provided a model of the virtues that Jesus taught.

In her 1234 letter to Agnes, she paid tribute to "so great and good a Lord, then, on coming into the Virgin's womb, chose to appear despised, needy, and *poor* in this world" (*Early Documents*, p. 36). Five years later, Clare explained to Agnes, "I am speaking of Him / Who is the Son of the Most High, / Whom the Virgin brought to birth / and remained a virgin after His birth" (p. 45). Jesus became incarnate because of Mary's willing assent.

Images of the Christmas and Easter mysteries recur in Clare's writing. In each case, Clare holds Mary up for imitation along with her son, Jesus. In the chapter of the rule on reception to the Poor Ladies, Clare writes, "I admonish, beg, and exhort my sisters to always wear cheap garments out of love of the most holy and beloved Child Who was wrapped in such poor little swaddling clothes and laid in a manger and of His most holy Mother" (*Early Documents*, p. 64). Writing to Ermentrude, Clare portrays the Passion of Christ and the mystery of Redemption: "Meditate constantly on the mysteries of the cross / and the agonies *of His Mother standing at the foot of the cross*" (p. 52).

In visualizing the central truths of Christianity, Clare points to both Jesus and Mary as examples of poverty and humility. Clare concludes her rule with the admonition that "we may always observe the poverty and humility of our Lord Jesus Christ and of His most holy Mother and the Holy Gospel we have firmly promised" (*Early Documents*, p. 76).

> The author of the *Legend* is faithful to Clare's association of poverty with the poor Christ and his poor mother, for he tells that "she encouraged them in their little nest of poverty to be conformed to the poor Christ, Whom a poor Mother placed as an infant in a narrow crib." (Peterson, *Clare of Assisi*, p. 268)

Pause: Ponder God's abundant grace that makes your soul a dwelling place of God.

Clare's Words

"The Salutation of the Blessed Virgin Mary," a litany of titles written by Saint Francis, reflects Clare's view of Mary in salvation history:

Hail, O Lady,
> holy Queen,
> Mary, holy Mother of God:
> you are the virgin made church
> and the one chosen by the most holy Father
>> in heaven

whom He consecrated
>with His most holy beloved Son
>and with the Holy Spirit the Paraclete,
in whom there was and is
>all the fullness of grace and every good.
Hail, His Palace!
Hail, His Tabernacle!
Hail, His Home!
Hail, His Robe!
Hail, His Servant!
Hail, His Mother!
And, [hail] all you holy virtues
>which through the grace and light of the holy Spirit
>are poured into the hearts of the faithful
>so that from their faithless state
>you may make them faithful to God.

>>>>(*Complete Works*, pp. 149–150)

Reflection

Mary, a young woman, became the bearer of the Savior of the world, Emmanuel, God-with-us. She symbolizes what Francis taught his followers: that God "created you and formed you to the image of His beloved Son according to the body, and to His likeness according to the spirit" (*Complete Works*, p. 29). All human beings are created to be God-bearers, to be God-with-us.

Clare honored Mary as a model of Jesus' poverty, humility, and charity, and she prayed that the creator of heaven and earth would come into the enclosure of our body. That a simple, innocent, Jewish girl from a poor village in a conquered country could become the mother of God proves that anything is possible with God.

✦ Clare saw every person as a dwelling place of God. Thus, she blessed the sisters saying, "Always be lovers of your souls and those of all your sisters" (*Early Documents*, p. 79). In what ways do you care for your soul? For the souls of others?

✧ Write a prayer that addresses the God who dwells within. In your prayer, express thanks, but also petition God for the spiritual growth you need to make your soul a worthy home for God.

✧ If helpful, visit a favorite Marian shrine or a place where you feel devotion to Mary. In any case, talk with Mary and thank her for bringing Jesus into the world. Ask her to help you bring the life of Jesus to your sisters and brothers.

✧ As you enter a room today, silently recall the dwelling of God inside you and in the people with whom you interact. If it helps, repeat the phrase, "This is indeed holy ground."

✧ Meditate on these stories about Mary: the birth of Jesus, Luke 2:1–20; the death of Jesus, John 19:17–30; Pentecost, Acts 1:12–14 and 2:1–4. Put yourself in Mary's shoes; ponder what she must have been feeling and thinking. Dialog with her about each of these key moments in her life and in the salvation of humankind.

✧ Pray that expectant mothers today may safely bear healthy babies and that they may love their children like Mary loved Jesus.

✧ As a "temple of God," how are you treating the body that the Creator gave you? Examine your conscience with these questions:
✦ What habits have I cultivated that honor the goodness of my body and keep it healthy?
✦ Do any of my habits misuse my body?
✦ How is my body a good servant to other people?
✦ How do I celebrate the gift of my body?
Ask God for the graces you need to keep your body a fit "temple" for the Spirit. Celebrate your body by taking a walk, going cross-country skiing, dancing, eating an orange, hugging someone you love—whatever fits your ability and fancy.

God's Word

It is not ourselves that we are proclaiming, but Christ Jesus . . . and ourselves as your servants for Jesus' sake. It is God who said, "Let light shine out of darkness," that has shone into our hearts to enlighten them with the knowledge of God's glory, the glory on the face of Christ. But we hold this treasure in pots of earthenware, so that the immensity of the power is God's and not our own. (2 Corinthians 4:5–7)

Closing prayer: God, creator of the sun, moon, stars, animals, insects, and birds, and maker of my own earthenware vessel, I cherish and celebrate your sacred presence within me.

CONTEMPLATION

✧ For Further Reading ✧

Armstrong, Regis J., ed. and trans. *Clare of Assisi: Early Documents*. Mahwah, NJ: Paulist Press, 1988.

Bartoli, Marco. *Clare of Assisi*. Translated by Frances Teresa. Quincy, IL: Franciscan Press, 1993.

Bodo, Murray. *Clare: A Light in the Garden*. Cincinnati: St. Anthony Messenger Press, 1992.

Carney, Margaret. *The First Franciscan Woman: Clare of Assisi and Her Form of Life*. Quincy, IL: Franciscan Press, 1993.

De Robeck, Nesta. *St. Clare of Assisi*. Chicago: Franciscan Herald Press, 1951.

Karper, Karen. *Clare: Her Light and Her Song*. Chicago: Franciscan Herald Press, 1987.

Miller, Ramona. *In the Footsteps of Saint Clare: A Pilgrim's Guide Book*. St. Bonaventure, NY: Franciscan Institute, 1993.

Peterson, Ingrid J. *Clare of Assisi: A Biographical Study*. Quincy, IL: Franciscan Press, 1993.

Acknowledgments *(continued)*

The excerpts on pages 15, 52–53, and 86 are from *St. Francis of Assisi, Writings and Early Biographies: English Omnibus of the Sources for the Life of St. Francis,* edited by Marion A. Habig (Chicago: Franciscan Herald Press, 1983), pages 370, 1332–1333, and 331, respectively. Copyright © 1983 by Franciscan Herald Press. Used with permission.

The excerpts on pages 18 (first excerpt), 18 (second and third excerpts), 20, 21, 24–25, 26, 27, 28 (first excerpt), 28 (second excerpt), 28 (third excerpt), 31 (first excerpt), 31 (second excerpt), 31–32, 32, 36, 36–37, 37, 37–38, 38, 41–42, 42–43, 43 (first excerpt), 43 (second excerpt), 47–48, 49 (first excerpt), 49 (second and third excerpts), 53–54, 54–55, 55, 57, 58 (first excerpt), 58 (second excerpt), 58 (third excerpt), 58–59, 59, 62 (first excerpt), 62 (second excerpt), 62 (third excerpt), 62 (fourth excerpt), 62 (fifth excerpt), 63, 66–67, 67–68, 72, 72–73, 73 (first excerpt), 73 (second excerpt), 74, 78 (first excerpt), 78 (second excerpt), 78 (third excerpt), 79 (first excerpt), 79 (second excerpt), 79 (third excerpt), 82–83, 83, 87–88, 89 (first excerpt), 94, 95 (first excerpt), 95 (second excerpt), 95 (third excerpt), 96 (third excerpt), 96 (fourth excerpt), 99–100, 100, 101, 101–102, 102 (first excerpt), 102 (second excerpt), 102–103, 106 (first excerpt), 106 (second excerpt), 106 (third excerpt), 107 (first excerpt), 107 (second excerpt), 107 (third excerpt), and 108 (second excerpt) are from *Clare of Assisi: Early Documents,* edited and translated by Regis J. Armstrong (Mahweh, NJ: Paulist Press, 1988), pages 165, 56, 56, 148, 157, 228–230, 57, 42, 189, 49, 55, 53, 63, 79, 44, 196–197, 36, 36–37, 35–36, 37, 48, 42, 44, 48–49, 211–212, 48, 217, 217, 57, 68–69, 79, 139, 67, 68, 74, 54, 63, 41, 144, 169, 40–42, 49, 52, 92–93, 71, 70, 56, 152, 53, 70, 134–135, 50, 58, 58, 58–59, 59, 203, 34, 105–106, 59, 136, 159, 168, 201, 165, 162, 205, 268–269, 40–41, 51–52, 62, 76, 55 and 58, 189, 36, 45, 64, 52, 76, and 79, respectively. Copyright © 1988 by the Province of St. Mary of the Capuchin Order. Used with permission.

The excerpt on page 19 and the fourth excerpt on page 107 are from *Clare of Assisi: A Biographical Study,* by Ingrid J. Peterson (Quincy, IL: Franciscan Press, 1993), pages 231 and 268. Copyright © 1993 by Franciscan Press. Used with permission.

Titles in the Companions for the Journey Series

Praying with Anthony of Padua

Praying with Benedict

Praying with C.S. Lewis

Praying with Catherine McAuley

Praying with Catherine of Siena

Praying with Clare of Assisi

Praying with Dominic

Praying with Dorothy Day

Praying with Elizabeth Seton

Praying with Francis of Assisi

Praying with Francis de Sales

Praying with Frédéric Ozanam

Praying with Hildegard of Bingen

Praying with Ignatius of Loyola

Praying with John Cardinal Newman

Praying with John of the Cross

Praying with Mother Teresa

Praying with Pope John the XXIII

Praying with Teresa of Ávila

Praying with Thérèse of Lisieux

Praying with Thomas Aquinas

Praying with Vincent de Paul

Order from your local religious bookstore or from

The Word Among Us Press
9639 Dr. Perry Rd., #126N
Ijamsville, Maryland, 21754
USA
1-800-775-9673
www.wordamongus.org

cla ra

lu ce cla ri or

Artwork by Clairvaux OSF

A BASIC CHRONOLOGY OF SAINT CLARE OF ASSISI

1193	Born to Ortulana and Favarone di Offreducio of noble class in Assisi
1199/1200	Clare's family flees to Perugia
1205	Family returns to Assisi
1210/11	Clare meets secretly with Francis concerning her vocation
1212	Palm Sunday night--Clare enters the Franciscan order; receives the tonsure at the Porziuncola
1212	Stays briefly at San Paolo in Bastia, and at Sant'Angelo di Panzo. By September, moves into San Damiano; Receives "form of life"
1215	Fourth Lateran Council; takes title "Abbess"
1216	Requests and receives the *Privilege of Poverty*
1218-19	The Rule of Hugolino
1219	Agnes sent to Monticello near Florence
1224	The beginning of the severe, long illness of Clare
1226	Francis dies; The funeral procession stops at San Damiano
1234	Clare's mother, Ortulana, joins the Poor Ladi First letter sent to Agnes of Prague
1234-39	Second and third letters sent to Agnes
1240	September - the repelling of the Saracens
1241	The liberation of the city of Assisi from Vitale d'Aversa
1247	Rule of Innocent IV made obligatory; Clare begins to write her own Rule
1252	Clare's Rule is approved through the cardinal protector, Cardinal Rainaldo
1253	The fourth letter sent to Agnes; The *Testament* of Clare; Agnes returns to San Damiano; Clare visited by Pope Innocent IV in late April
1253, Aug 9	Pope Inn. IV approves the Rule of Clare with the bull *"Solet Annure"*
1253, Aug 11	Clare dies at San Damiano
1254	Cardinal Rainaldo becomes Pope Alexander IV, canonizes Clare and designates San Giorgio as the site for her basilica
1260	Consecration of the Basilica of Santa Chiara